1992

Folk Jewelry of the World

GER DANIËLS

Folk Jewelry of the World

Foreword by Roelof Munneke

RIZZOLI
NEW YORK

First published in the United States of America in 1989 by
Rizzoli International Publications, Inc.
597 Fifth Avenue, New York, NY 10017

Simultaneously published in German by Ernst Wasmuth Verlag
GmbH & Co.
Copyright © 1989 Compartners B.V. Haarlem; Ger Daniëls,
Heemstede; and Ernst Wasmuth Verlag GmbH & Co., Tübingen

Library of Congress Cataloging-in-Publication Data

Daniëls, Ger.
[Schmuckformen der Völker, English]
Folk jewelry of the world / by Ger Daniëls : foreword by Roelof
Munneke.
p. cm.
Translation of: Schmuckformen der Völker.
ISBN 0-8478-1070-4
1. Ethnic jewelry-Catalogs. I. Title.
NK4890.E86D3613 1989
739.27-dc 19

Printed and bound in Spain

Preface

Traditional costumes help to distinguish oneself from others outside the community and emphasize the ties of fellowship within the community. These costumes subsist on the belief that the interests uniting the members of a community are stronger than the interests which separate them.

This is an important point, if we are trying to understand the changes in clothing, jewelry and other body decoration over the last century. The twentieth century has become the century of communication and information. There has been such spectacular discovery and consequent advancement in air and ground transportation, and in radio, television, telephone and computer technology that almost no community remains isolated from the rest of the world. On the level of the nation state many traditional ideals and roles can not be handled sensibly any longer, since loyalty to a community, expressed in national costume and in numerous aspects of body decoration, is increasingly detached from the primary interests of the individual and the state.

Today, in the last decade of the twentieth century, traditional body decoration and costumes belong to the past. They are folklore. If these costumes still play a role in everyday life, they are worn primarily by women. At this time, men are still predominantly the first to leave home, to open up new economic possibilities, and to face the norms of the omnipotent community to which they belong. Frequently, adjusting to the values and external forms of a new community seems more promising than adhering to those of the original community. In most cases the women are left at home, and therefore become involved in a rearguard action against the rapidly approaching outer world.

Regarding all the changes in traditional body decoration, we must not forget that the outward appearance not only reflects ideals, but a way of life. In short, it is connected with society as a whole. If, due to changes in the sociocultural context, distinctive traditional values, norms and ideals are no longer nourished, they will die along with the finely structured and far-reaching roots connecting them to society. The external forms of certain traditions, too, will then disappear sooner or later. If a traditional community of life is destroyed — for example, if most men, working as day laborers, are away from home most of the year — this must have consequences on the continuity and the functioning of that society. In his book Ger Daniëls, thanks to his perseverance and his eye for detail, has brought within the reach of a broad public many of the outward characteristics which link people from former times to the culture from which these characteristics originated. The fact that the function and significance of the decoration in contemporary context is unclear in many cases, and will probably remain so, is tragic but irreversible.

The illustrations in the form of drawings have the advantage of omitting unimportant details from the subject's environment. Thus the different pieces of jewelry and decoration are given the attention they deserve.

Dr. Roelof Munneke,
Curator, Department of African and Islamic Culture,
National Museum of Ethnology,
Leiden, Holland, December 1988.

Introduction

People decorate themselves: they change their appearance with headdresses, clothing, tattoos and painting to make themselves more beautiful. They also adorn themselves for other purposes, but the principal reason is to be beautiful.

Changes in the outward appearance of man can be found all over the world and the manner in which it is accomplished is frequently the same. However, there are many differences, too, since the beauty ideals of one people may be very different from another. This is the case between neighboring countries and within one's own nation. The tattoo, for example, an adornment of the body which can be found in all parts of the world, is — at least in the West — not to everyone's liking. The same applies to a higher degree to skull deformation or to nose, ear or lip plugs (Ill. 181).

Nevertheless, an unbiased attitude toward beauty ideals of other nations is necessary for the understanding of the text and illustrations in this book. It goes back only some hundred years, and is confined to cultures in which jewelry and adornments played an important role — and in some cases still do today.

It would be impossible to present all peoples of the world here, together with their traditional jewelry, their tattoos and paintings. For this reason the book cannot be complete, and does not pretend to be. It is intended as an introduction into an immense field; some countries are dealt with in detail (although not completely), others scarcely or not at all.

For the illustrations, drawings have been chosen, elaborated on the basis of photographs, sketches or engravings. In this way the illustrative material is as homogeneous as possible.

Definition

Archaeological discoveries reveal that people have always adorned themselves. The wish to change oneself positively, to distinguish oneself, or to show which group one belongs to is as old as mankind itself.

In primitive races, decoration protects oneself from evil powers. The amulet protects against evil, illness and sorcery; the talisman is thought to bring good luck.

For many people in Western society today jewelry is a sign of wealth and extravagance; a piece of jewelry's luster, price, and rarity of stones plays an important role in helping people make their choice as to what to wear. There is a great discrepancy between the amulet, talisman and ritual body painting of the primitive races, and the jewelry that symbolizes status and wealth of modern people. For the people of Tibet, Mongolia, Turkmenistan, and Northwest Africa, who frequently lead a nomadic life, the value of a piece of jewelry as talisman or amulet and its religious meaning is as important as its material worth. A richly adorned wife shows that she comes from a wealthy family and contributes as much to her husband's prestige as a herd of cattle.

Adornments or changes in the outward appearance can be either permanent or temporary. Permanent adornments are tattoos, scar tattoos, elongations of the skull or neck, filing of the teeth, inlaid work in the teeth and piercing of the wing of the nose or the nasal septum, of the ear-lobe, external ear edges, lips, tongue, and cheeks. Temporary adornments are body painting, dying of hair, fingernails, teeth and beards, and epilation of the body hair and the eyebrows. Hairstyle, with false hair, wigs, or headdresses as possibilities, is also not permanent. The same applies to veils, loin cloths and penis quivers.

Finally there is decoration of the body, with amulets, strings of beads, finger or toe rings, necklaces, bracelets or ankle bands, pendants, belts, pins, nose rings and earrings as well as lip plugs. Some of these articles are permanent in the sense that they are worn day and night; others imply a permanent body deformation, such as lip plugs, nose rings and earrings. An inevitably permanent defromation is created by the neck rings which lead to an elongation of the neck (Ill. 49).

Categories

Categories of jewelry can be distinguished. There are pieces of jewelry with a protective function, such as amulets, and pieces indicating social status, rank, age, tribe or origin. Moreover, there are those representing a certain capital like family property or dowry. These pieces are manufactured, in general, of rare or precious materials, often with complicated and time-intensive manufacturing techniques. Some jewelry is worn only for celebrations, marriage for example, and borrowed from the trustee of the family estate for the duration of the festivities. The fourth catagory is solely decorative, even if this cannot always be said definitely. Most of these pieces are not very precious.

Materials and Technique

Jewelry is often manufactured from different materials, and there are many possible reasons for using a specific one. First, it must be available. Other than that, beauty, color, plasticity, processing possibilities, value, and symbolic meaning all play an important role.

A. United States, c. 1870. Breast ornament of silver alloy of the South Plains Indians.

7

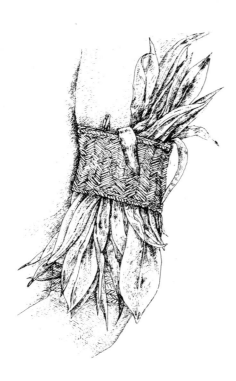

B. Papua New Guinea. Bracelet for the upper arm made of plaiting leaves.

Materials are taken from plants — flowers, leaves, grasses, fibers, bamboo, bast, wood, seeds, kernels, amber, and dyestuffs; animals — hair, tails, feathers, wool, the shield of insects, tortoise-shells, shells, claws, bills, teeth, skulls, horns, ivory, bones, and unique features such as porcupine bristles; and minerals — clay, metals like aluminum, copper, silver or gold; precious and semiprecious stones; simply "beautiful" stones; and similar gems. These materials are often available nearby, sometimes acquired by barter. In many cases they are brought from far away.

It would be impossible to describe all manufacturing techniques of jewelry. Two will be mentioned here: those of shell and metal.

Working with shells requires much patience and skill. Using a bamboo drill turned between the hands and continuously adding sand and water, one bores a hole into the shell. Bamboo is used as well for sawing. On a quartziferous marl block the material is finally polished. To produce a flat ring with a diameter of eight inches, thirty-five working hours are necessary on average. Many pieces of jewelry are produced of gold, silver, copper, or various metal alloys. Different techniques can be applied in their production. Metal plates or sheets can be obtained by first melting the material, then casting it into a flat mold, and finally hardening it with a hammer on an anvil. From this material forms can be cut out, that may be further processed or used as background for ornaments. Thin sheets can also be bent into the desired shape and then soldered together. In this way simple items can be produced, like amulet cases or hollow crosses (see Mauretania and South Morocco, Ills. 143, 144). The metal can also be wrought into the desired form by processing it with different hammers. Relief forms are possible as well. Here the piece is laid on a matrix built on the ground and vaulted inward or outward and then hammered. A completely different technique is *à cire perdue* ("lost form"). First the smith makes a wax model which is covered with clay. The clay cover is hardened in the sun and/or burnt in live coals. The wax melts and

flows from the form into a basin with cold water, so that it can be used again. In the meantime the smith has molten the metal which is poured into the mold. When it has cooled, it is broken — thus the term "lost form" — revealing the image within. Every piece therefore is unique. The item is then cooked some time in a saline solution. The sulphureous oxidation disappears and the piece of jewelry begins to shine. Finally it is filed, polished, and perhaps engraved. The silver crosses in illustrations 146 and 147 as well as the massive earrings of the Tuareg (Ills. 146, 148) have been produced with this technique, in contrast to the crosses from Mauretania which are hollow. Sand forms are used as well. The desired form is pressed into wet sand and molten metal poured into the indentation.

Metal is often used as wire, in particular for jewelry made of silver or gold. Long, thin strips are cut from a metal plate and then processed by hammering, planing, and rolling. To obtain a thin and even wire, the strip is pulled with the help of pliers through a plate with holes of different sizes and shapes . Afterward the wire is often twisted, ridged or braided with others to form a thick rope. Wire is used both for filigree work and for clasps. Filigree is possible both with or without a background. In the case of the amulet cases from Tibet (Ills. 86, 87, and 89 among others) and the cross from South Morocco (Ill. 144), filigree has been applied to a background of silver sheet. When wire is not soldered onto a background but shows openings in the material for the passage of light, it is called *à jouré* work. This technique is used, for example, for earrings (Ill. 26). When globules are used instead of wire, this is termed granulation. In the case of the earrings in illustration 26 granulation technique was used as well as filigree. These two techniques are combined very often. Actually, the term "filigree" is composed of the Latin terms *filum*, "wire," and *granum*, "grain."

General techniques to decorate a metal with motifs are chasing, punching and engraving. Chasing means the chiseling of figures. In the case of punching, small circles, triangles, or other designs on a punch machine are punched into the piece of jewelry to create patterns or ornamental borders. Engraving is the technique with greatest variability. By means of the engraving iron or chisel the desired figures are engraved into the metal.

C. New Ireland, c. 1900. Kapkap ornament, tortoise-shell on shell.

Colors can be applied to a piece of jewelry by attaching stones, beads or glass, but there is a specific technique, enameling, to obtain colored metal. Glass colored by metallic oxide is founded on a metal surface; chromium oxide, for example, creates a green coloration, and cuprous oxide, blue. The glass is pulverized, distributed on the metal jewelry to be colored, and burnt into it. This is possible since the melting point of enamel is slightly lower than that of metal. Not all metals can be used in this technique; principally silver and brass are employed. Enamel can also be cast in ridges (*email champlevé*) or burnt into a part of the jewelry surrounded with wire, with the wires remaining visible. In particular the Kabyles (Ills. 136, 137) and the Moroccans (Ills. 151, 154, 167) use this technique.

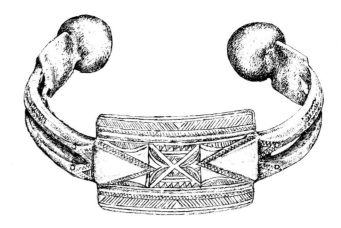

E. South Morocco and Mauretania, twentieth century. Silver ankle band.

D. Left: Thail and early twentieth century, silver bracelet decorated with silver wire. Right: Burma, early twentieth century, silver bracelet decorated with silver wire (see illustrations 42 and 44).

position, he was permanently threatened by spirits living in the interior of the earth.

This is not an isolated belief; many peoples considered the processing of metal and in particular its exploitation in mines a dangerous business: the interior of the earth was not to be destroyed on any account. The Mongolians, for example, had hardly any mines, although their country was rich in minerals. Silver for their jewelry was imported from China.

Global Parallels in Body Decoration
This clearly demonstrates that jewelry and other decorations of the body reveal not only something about an individual (dowry, social status, tribe affiliation), but also about a nation and its history and culture. The migration of nations and consequent reciprocal cultural influence — such as the spreading of religion and the role of magic — may all be perceived through this ornamentation. Travelers took their

The *niello* technique is very similar to enameling. A piece of jewelry is engraved. Then an alloy of silver, copper, lead and sulphur of borax is pulverized and — mixed with ammonium chloride — applied into the ridges. After this etching process, a blue-black drawing on a silver background is visible. Good examples are illustrations 150 and 162, both from Morocco. Jewelry made of silver or other metals is gold-plated, too. For this purpose gold is mixed with mercury: this mixture has a considerably lower melting point than gold. The clean silver is at first treated with mercury, nitric acid and water in order to ensure a good binding. Then the gold mixture is applied. The whole piece is slowly heated, so that the mixture evaporates, leaving a thin, permanent gold layer behind on the silver (Ills. 119–131).

Metal was processed by a smith, who enjoyed great esteem. Most peoples associated the smith with the supernatural. The Turkish tribes in Central Asia, for example, believed that raw metals came from the bowels of Mother Earth, where they developed in the course of time into finished metal. The smith was a substitute for Mother Earth; his oven, an artificial womb, gave birth to the metal. The smith, the master of fire, was thought to have power over time, since he accelerated this birth. His soul could resist the fire; thus he was invulnerable. He had healing power and could read the future. On the other hand, due to his special

F. Central Asia, mid- to late-nineteenth century. Tekke Turkmen asyk (see illustrations 123 and 124).

manner of dress and decoration to other lands. When different peoples made contact, directly or indirectly, they sometimes adopted certain elements of decoration: materials, motifs, or customs. Thus parallels in body decoration developed all over the world.

The fact that there are numerous analogies is demonstrated by some examples. The Mangbetu in Zaire elongated their skulls by the wrapping technique (Ills. 174, 177). This custom can be found everywhere, using not only the wrapping technique but another method as well: the skull of the child was jammed between two small boards which were bound together. One board was laid on the forehead, the other on the back of the head. By pulling tightly the skull was squeezed together, resulting in a longer profile and, when seen from the front, a broader face. Skull deformation is a custom with a long tradition. In ancient Egypt and Europe this custom was already popular. In the ancient world the elongation of the head was mostly reserved for distinguished or free persons; slaves were not allowed to use this technique, so that the social status of an individual was literally visible. In the Americas excavations reveal the existence of deformed skulls for the first millennium before our era. Today the wrapping technique is still practiced (or has been practiced until recently) in Zaire as well as Melanesia and New Britain. The technique using the small boards is still employed by the Shipibo Indians in East Peru and by the Nootka and Kwakiutl Indians, at the Northwest coast of Canada, among others.

Deformation and painting of the teeth still exists in different parts of the world. There are four methods to change one's teeth: extraction, filing, inlaid work and painting. The Naga (Ill. 52) and the Dayak, for example, paint their teeth black. In particular in Africa and Indonesia, but also in other places, teeth are filed as well as decorated with inlaid work. Especially in Africa teeth are extracted — a custom which is connected with the initiation ceremonies of young men. In this way they proved their insensitivity to pain. In such a culture a man with a complete set of teeth was not considered a full member! As with the filing and decoration by inlaid work, this custom has not yet disappeared completely.

The piercing of the earlobe and external ear edges, the wing of the nose, the nasal septum and the lips is found very often. The piercing of one or more holes in the earlobe is completely acceptable for the Western world; but the unproportionally long earlobes found, for example, in Kalimantan (Ills. 32 and 34) may be difficult to appreciate. The initial steps are taken in childhood to obtain such big holes in the earlobes or lips. The first small rod or ring is replaced after some time by a bigger plug or a heavier ring and this is continued until the desired size has been obtained. The wooden plates worn by the Sara women in their lips (by the way, the woman in illustration 181 is wearing film cases in her lips!) are among the largest that exist. In size they resemble that worn by the Botocudo Indians in Brazil, who even owe their name to the *botoques*, the Portuguese word for the wooden plates worn in the underlip or earlobes. Lip plugs and lip ornaments are almost unknown in Asia and Oceania. The Papuans, for example, pierce their ears and nose, but not their lips. When they are fighting, however, they carry ornamental plates between their teeth, set with the large tusks of wild boars.

Tattoos and scar tattoos as well as the painting of the body and the face are also widespread. Peoples with dark skin practice scar tattoos; this manner of skin decoration has been developed most by the peoples in Central Africa (Ills. 175, 176, 182). Those with fairer skin use tattoos. Both kinds of tattoos are practiced among some peoples by both sexes, while among others only by one sex or the other. The lengthy operations creating the desired drawings are frequently performed during puberty and often have more than an aesthetic purpose. Tattoos can also be added later; for example, after wars with other peoples, as a sort of "war decoration" (see illustration 50), where two human figures represent the heads which this man has cut off. Sometimes designs which were originally used for tattoos survive in drawings on clothes or in engravings on jewelry. Good examples are the two Naga boys (Ill. 51) and the "mola," the blouse from Panama (Ill. 203). The motifs on the Chilcat shawl (Ill. 222), too, seems to be related to the tattoos which the Indians of the Northwest coast of Canada carried on breast and arms. These are only some examples, but it has to be supposed that many motifs on pieces of jewelry and clothes were originally motifs of tattoos or paintings. Thus it is possible that even the simplest engraving on a piece of jewelry has a deeper sense not known by the person wearing it.

Global Parallels in Materials

As aforementioned, many of the materials used for jewelry can be found all over the world. The cowrie shell, for example, exists in many regions of the earth. Apart from its use as jewelry this shell is employed as means of payment. The cowrie shell can be found not only in coastal regions, but also in Central Africa, in the Hindu Kush (Ill. 71), with the Naga (Ill. 51), and Akha (Ill. 46). Other shells, too, are used for jewelry in regions far away from their places of origin and because of their scarcity are especially valued. In the Himalayas, for example, in particular in Ladakh, the women wear shell bracelets.

Red coral is one of the most widely used and popular materials. Ancient Chinese documents report on the value of red coral and the resulting flourishing trade. Many centuries later Marco Polo reported how much red coral was esteemed in the Far East. In Tibet, Mongolia, and other regions of Central Asia red coral has been one of the most popular elements used in jewelry for a long time, not only with respect to headdresses, necklaces, rosaries, rings and bracelets, but also weapons. Red coral is not native to any of these countries and was imported. In particular corals from the

G. Tibet, c. 1900. Silver pin with turquoise.

Mediterranean countries were much sought after.

Red is usually the color of good luck and success. In many European countries as well red coral is very popular; the same applies to North Africa. The Kabyles in Algeria, for example, hang a small coral twig around the neck of children as a protective amulet. Corals are not only said to protect someone from mischief, but also to have a favorable influence on the milk flow of nursing mothers. A coral twig in the form of a horn is believed to enhance male fertility. Large pieces of coral are used for the jewelry of the Kabyles. If this is too expensive, a substitute is employed which resembles the coral as much as possible, such as red celluloid.

This custom is typical: in all regions where precious stones or beads are believed to have magic power, they are replaced by cheaper materials which resemble them as nearly as possible, in particular in color. This applies especially to amber. In Africa, above all in the north, west and northeast, amber is very popular, worn as a necklace or braided into the hair (Ills. 149, 186). Due to financial reasons copal from Zanzibar is used often as a substitute, as well as ambroid which is made by compressing small pieces of amber together. Thus ambroid is also amber, but it does not possess the subtlety of the large pieces. As a substitute for real amber beads, beads of bakelite or plastics are worn frequently. Where amber is mentioned in the illustrations, it may be that actually one of the other materials is used, which, however, has the same qualities for the wearer as those attributed to amber.

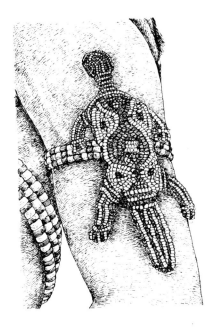

H. Zaïre, c. 1960. Bead bracelet for the upper arm of a Luba dancer of Cabinda.

Real amber is a fossil resin from extinct coniferous trees that existed in temperate climatic zones and in subtropical forests some forty to sixty million years ago. Amber has been found in countries bordering the Baltic Sea, on or near the Swedish, Danish, German, Polish and Russian coasts. As jewelry it has been found in graves in France and Spain dating from the period between 15,000 and 10,000 B.C. Around 3000 B.C. the peoples of the Baltic countries exported amber to almost all European countries, and by the thirteenth to the eighteenth century amber beads were produced in Europe

for Catholic, Buddhist and Islamic rosaries. Thus it is not astonishing that the German farmer's wife (Ill. 238), the Berber women (Ills. 145, 149, 150, 156, 157, 159, 163) and women from Mauretania (Ills. 142, 143) all wore amber from the Baltic region — and still wear it today.

Amber is said not only to protect against the evil eye, but also to have healing power. For this reason it is frequently worn in the Arabian world. In Tibet, Mongolia, China and neighboring regions amber is often combined with corals and turquoise. Red coral symbolizes blood, fire and light, blue turquoise, water, sky and air, and amber, the earth. The red variant was imported from Burma. These three stones were not only used to decorate people, but also the statues of gods, which often are richly ornamented.

The turquoise, too, is said to protect against mischief and to have healing power. It can be found in many parts of the earth; in Ladakh (Ills. 69, 70), many turquoises are fixed on the *perak,* the headdress of women. This stone is used frequently and is very popular all over Central Asia and in the Middle East. This is not true for China, however. There, women would never wear the turquoise. In North America the turquoise is often worn by the Hopi, Zuni and Navajo Indians. In Asia alone there were mines in Tibet and China, but in particular the Turquoise mines of Meshed in Persia (now Iran) were famous. Some followers of the ancient Bon religion and other religions, where shamans played a role, believed that they had two souls, a breath soul and a shadow soul. The latter, termed *la,* could leave the body temporarily. Some Tibetans believed that their *la* was in a turquoise which they wore around their necks. We cannot go into detail here, but in view of what we have said about the red coral and amber it should be clear how closely beliefs as well as beauty are associated with jewelry.

It is impossible to enumerate all beads or stones, but glass beads should be mentioned. From the beginning of the fifteenth century they were spread from Europe over the entire world, at first by explorers and later by merchants. Beads were very popular, in particular in North America and in Africa. Beside the small colored glass beads, large multicolored ones were exported from Europe, such as the Venetian glass much sought after in Africa. Although even the ancient Egyptians manufactured this kind of beads, it is supposed that the majority of the old beads found in Africa came from Europe a long time ago.

Thus, the materials with which people adorn themselves have come into all parts of the earth due to commerce, migration of nations, or the spreading of different religions, together with the materials, the manufacturing techniques, motifs and symbolic meaning. Therefore, it may happen that in some cultures a particular piece of jewelry is worn which, although in common in the distant past in another culture, has since disappeared in that culture. An example are the *fibulas,* pins from ancient Mediterranean cultures still worn in North Africa today. They are dealt with in the illustrations from Algeria and Morocco.

Global Parallels in Customs and Motifs

There are numerous similar customs, too. The German farmer's wife in illustration 238, for example, is wearing a high hat, definitely an attribute of a married woman. The same custom is shown in illustration 157 and 159, where the difference between an unmarried and a married Haddidu Berber woman is visible. The latter is wearing a pointed quiver on her head, which is covered with a handkerchief and re-

I. South China, twentieth century. Hairstyle of Miao woman.

sembles a high pointed cap. The Druse (Ill. 135) had a similar custom. Here, on the evening of the marriage, the bridegroom puts a conical silver quiver on the bride's head, up to 18 inches high. This quiver was worn by the bride her entire life. Over the quiver a long veil hung down, with which she could cover herself. The illustration from Palestine (Ill.134) shows the fez, called *shatweh*, richly ornamented with coins as the dowry. In Greece one can find a headdress worn as a diadem, but which formerly — during the reign of the Turks — was attached to the fez. This decoration is a gift of the bridegroom, too. In Turkmenistan married women wear an *egme* on their high headdresses, a slightly bent silver plate which is beautifully shaped and partially gold-plated (Ills. 121, 122, 123). It is also reserved for married women; the girls are wearing caps. The same applies to the Akha in Burma and Thailand (Ill. 46). The similarity of the Ait Haddidu in Morocco is astonishing. The horn-shaped headdress of the Khalkha Mongolians (Ills. 97, 98, 99, 100) is also worn only by married women.

With the headdress of the Khalkha Mongolians we come to the frequently used horn motif, which is also widespread. It can be found in the Tibetan headdresses (Ills. 72, 73, 74) or in China, with the Miao among others; moreover, with the Ifugao on the Philippines (together with the head of the hornbill, Ill. 24); on various islands of the Indonesian archipelagos, with the Toradja and the Dayak; with the

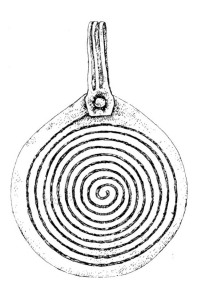

J. Southwest Morocco, twentieth century. A spiral design made by niello *technique. Ait Ba Amrane (see illustration 150).*

Naga in India and Burma (Ills. 54, 56) (together with the feathers of the hornbill); but also in Africa and from time to time with the North American Indians. Apart from headdresses, the horn is employed as an ornament, on fabrics, in engravings or as tattoos (Ill. 57).

Along with the buffalo horn the ram horn was employed as a pattern as well. In hethitic writing the spiral led back to the ram horn. The double spiral on the pins in illustration 64, the earrings from Nias (Ill. 35) and of the Karo Batak (Ill. 27), clearly originates from this horn. The macrocosmic spiral is one of the oldest archetypes developed spontaneously from a motoric gesture. The motif is associated with the sun, the moon, fertility, and with all cycles. In various cultures it is also associated with the snake, the whirlpool, or the curly tail of animals. In particular the snake spiral is widespread and for many peoples the symbol of wisdom and eternity.

K. Mongolia, c. 1900. Silver bracelets: two dragons fighting for the jewel.

The spiral is probably the archetype of the circle. For the Buddhist peoples the circle symbolizes the "wheel of law," the cycle of life and death, birth and rebirth. The amulet cases (Ills. 86, 87, 93, 105) often resemble the front of a prayer wheel: if it is turned, a connection to the gods is established. Concentric circles, several circles around the same center, are closely connected with birth and rebirth. The pointed ornaments on the diadem of the Berber woman of the Ait Ba Amran (Ill. 150) contain also concentric circles. Here they are a symbol for the sun. The sun between two mythic animals, in this case dragons, is shown by the silver ornament in illustration 90. Bracelets inspired by this motif can be found in different Asian countries. Dragons are connected with water and clouds and thus with rain and fertility. The origin of the dragon goes back to the snake cults. Another important mythic animal, which has already been mentioned in short, is the hornbill. The Dayak believe it to be the god of the upper world, whereas the watersnake is the god of the underworld. The spiral motifs used for tattoos as well as for ear decoration, bead ornaments and other items, originated in both gods (Ills. 30, 31, 32, 33).

In many countries the hornbill is the symbol of the brave war bird; it plays an important role in Africa, the Himalayas and Southeast Asia. Many African tribes use the bill of this bird for war decoration, or a copy of the bird's head, cut in wood, is worn on the head. The feathers have an important symbolic meaning: all over Southeast Asia only those warriors who had captured a human head were allowed to wear the beautiful long tail-feathers in their headdresses. In some Naga tribes (Ills. 54 and 56) and among the Dayak (Ill. 33) the number of feathers allowed depended on the number of heads captured. Moreover, the hornbill was also a kind of soul leader. In the Batak as well as the Ao and the Konyak Naga, coffins often have its form. The Batak believed that the bird was to lead the dead to their future home.

The feathers and bill of this bird are often used together with buffalo horns. These are often copied by using thin metal or wood. Thus both the buffalo and the hornbill were closely connected to the war and death cult. Although the symbolic meaning of these decorations was very important, the items remained ornamental in the sense that they were intended to enhance the beauty of man. Much more could be written about the reasons for certain motifs or materials. To keep to the terminology used thus far, the book reveals only a "tip of the veil" — an introduction to the immeasurable treasure of the "jewels of the people." It is not only a book to be read, but above all, a visual gem.

December 1988
Ger Daniëls

Description of the illustrations

Illustration 1. Maori, New Zealand, *c.* 1875.
Nga Hua, a wife of King Tuahaio, in the last quarter of the nineteenth century wore jewelry made of green jade. In her ear she had a shark tooth, covered with red sealing-wax. Around her neck she wore a *hei-tiki* made of jade. *Hei* means "pendant." and *tiki* refers to the "human kind," i.e. the presentation of man in general. The *hei-tiki* was for the Maori a souvenir of one or more deceased ancestors, who passed this piece of jewelry from one generation to the next. Thus the *hei-tiki* had a high value: The jewelry established the connection to the *mana* (magic power) of the ancestors. Like most valuable things, the *hei-tikis* had their own names, too, but most of them have been forgotten. Today *hei-tiki* means "talisman." In former times it was worn both by men and women, later (and also today) only by women.
Hei-tikis are not in any case a fertility symbol, although many of them portray the fair sex. Maori carvings in general abound in sexual symbolism. The carving of a *hei-tiki* requires a lot of work. The material used is tough and hard. It is called "nephrite" (New Zealand jade) and was found in the riverbeds of the Teremakau and Arahura on the West coast of the South Island. The Maoris were — like the ancient Chinese — experts in the color and structure of jade, and they had names for each different kind; the green-yellow type, for example, was called *kahurangi*, which means "garment of heaven." The carving of a *hei-tiki* requires about 500 to 1000 hours of work, depending on its size.
Contrary to the Maori men, who had tattoos all over their faces, the women had tattoos only on their lips and chin and sometimes between their eyes.

Illustration 2. New Zealand, nineteenth century or earlier.
Hei-tiki made of jade, with eyes inlaid with shells.

Illustration 3. Australia, Arnhemland, 1947.
The ribbon the young girl is wearing round her head is decorated with six crocodile teeth. Although the girl is very young, she is already a bride; early marriage is very common. Ribbons for the head, ornamented with teeth (*tiaras*) have a long tradition all over Australia. In Central Australia ribbons with kangaroo teeth were worn both by men and women. More than 4000-year-old graves have been discovered, where skulls have been found with a great number of teeth, incisors of marsupials, on their forehead. As regards even older discoveries (*c.* 6000 years) similar ornaments, necklaces composed of teeth, have been found.

Illustration 4. Near the Kimberley Plateau, Northwest Australia, late nineteenth century.
This mother-of-pearl pendant shows one of the major motifs used by the Aborigines, an entwined pattern engraved into the shell.
Afterward red ocher was rubbed into the carvings. This beautiful pendant was produced somewhere on the coast of Kimberley. In the ceremonial exchange of gifts objects made of mother-of-pearl were highly esteemed; similar pendants have been found far from their place of production, namely at the Great Australian Bight.

Illustration 5. Owa Raha, Solomon Islands/Melanesia, 1932.
Man from Hupans with a ribbon of shells around his head. The ornament in his nose, made of shells, is a status symbol, since only chieftains and their families wore such pieces in their pierced nasal septum.
In these regions both men, women and children wore much jewelry produced of shells, plant seeds, animal teeth, flowers (mainly hibiscus) or tortoise-shell. In particular shells and tortoise-shell were carefully processed. Strings composed of animal teeth or shells were often used as means of payment. The headband with white shells shown here is very precious, since these shells cannot be found near the islands, but were acquired by barter.
The ornament in his nose is made of a disk of the tridacna shell, which was ground internally by a special method. The motifs take their pattern from the stylized frigate bird. Sometimes a stylized fish was used. This piece is of great significance; thus it would certainly not be employed as means of payment.

Illustration 6 and 7. Solomon Islands, early twentieth century.
Two breast pendants made of shells. Both pendants show four frigate birds. In the Pacific region these birds have the same significance as the hornbill in Southeast Asia (see introduction as well as the Philippines, illustrations 24, 25; Sarawak, illustration 30; and Naga, illustration 54). Here, too, the bird is accompanying the soul into the kingdom of death. If the frigate bird is seen during the obsequies, this is a good sign, since it will take the soul of the deceased with it. Illustration 11 shows the bird more clearly.

Illustration 8. Solomon Islands, early twentieth century.
This man from Malaita is wearing a necklet consisting of many threaded dog teeth. Ear and nose rings are made of a tridacna shell. Since the 1920s the custom was adopted from the inhabitants of Santa Cruz to combine mother-of-pearl with motifs sawn from tortoise-shell. The tortoise-shell motifs were attached to the front side of the shell. This influence is also visible in the crescent-shaped ornament with a bird motif of tortoise-shell worn by this inhabitant of the Solomon Islands.

Illustration 9. Santa Cruz Islands, early twentieth century.
A man with hair dyed blond, an ear ornament of tortoise-shell and a bracelet on the upper arm made of plaited plant fibers. The most precious piece of jewelry he is wearing is the breast ornament, consisting of tridacna shell and a motif of tortoise-shell: in the middle a stylized frigate bird and above it two rows with similar stylized dolphins (or other fishes).

Illustration 10. Santa Cruz Islands.
Variant of the breast ornament in illustration 9.

Illustration 11. Engraved shell from Malaita, Solomon Islands.
Such shells were worn on the forehead.

Illustration 12. Papua New Guinea, 1953.
This man from the Central Mountains, east of Mount Hagen, is wearing a headdress containing feathers of the bird of paradise. Only the cock of this species has such feathers; the female is inconspicuous.

At the beginning of this century it looked as if the bird of paradise would become extinct. The feathers were very popular in Europe and thus were an important export. Fortunately, the shooting of the male bird of paradise was officially forbidden as early as 1920.

As well as the red feathers of the large bird of paradise the man in the illustration is wearing a turquoise-colored breastplate made from a different species of bird of paradise, the *Lophorina superba feminina.* Through the nose he is wearing feathers of the "King of Saxony," also a bird of paradise. On the forehead and the nose, shell ornaments have been attached. The crescent-shaped, gold-colored shells on the chin and around the neck are precious pieces, coming from islands of the Torres Strait. These shells were transported a long way until they reached the hardly accessible mountainous country.

Illustration 13. Indonesia, West Irian, twentieth century.
A nose ornament made of bones of the Asmat Papuans, worn through the nasal septum at ceremonies. In most cases it is produced from pork bones, but sometimes also from human.

Illustration 14. Papua New Guinea, early twentieth century.
Roro woman from the Southeast (the region on the Gulf of Papua) dressed for a dance honoring the birth of a first child. This young woman lived at the beginning of this century. But today people still decorate themselves in a fantastic way. Regional differences with regard to body decoration are vast and many things have been lost over time. Especially the area around the Central Mountains near Mount Hagen is very famous for its tradition of wearing magnificent headdresses.

The body of the woman illustrated is decorated with different kinds of ornaments. Apart from perishable material such as leaves, flowers and fibers, shells, tortoise-shells, feathers and teeth were used. The circular pieces of the tridacna-shell, on which polished ornaments sawn out of tortoise-shells are fixed, occur in different regions of Melanesia. They are mainly breast ornaments called *kapkap.*

The long ornament on the breast shows the high social status of the one who wears it. It consists of two rows of disks made of wild boar's tusks. The woman's bracelets are produced from the middle piece of a cone shell. The big red feathers are those of a bird of paradise.

Tattoos as well as body painting were typical for these regions; some people were even tattooed all over.

Illustration 15. Papua New Guinea, 1934.
This splendid headdress is also worn in the region of the woman in illustration 14. Mekeo men still wear these gigantic ornaments on their heads. Here again the big feathers of a bird of paradise crown the ornament and form a nice contrast to the brighter feathers, which are cut in such a way that they resemble those of the "King of Saxony," mentioned in illustration . 12. The big round middle piece of the headdress consists of carefully cut feathers. The ribbon around the man's head is made of several shields of the scarabaeus. On the man's breast an ornament of wild boar's tusks is visible, and in his nose a bone of the cassowary (a local running bird).

Illustration 16. Micronesia, Caroline Islands, 1900.
A young woman from Migiul with bracelets of coconut shells, flowers at her ears and a necklace of hibiscus fiber dyed black. The most characteristic dress was the long wide skirt reaching down to the floor, made of grasses and the leaves of different trees and plants, cut with a shell into strips of different lengths and widths.

Illustration 17. Micronesia, Truk Islands, 1900.
The earlobes of these women are very long. Again and again new shell rings are put into the pierced earlobe, so that the hole becomes larger and larger. The whole earlobe is decorated with little earrings, and strings of larger shell rings hang at the edges of their ears. The women wear strings of coconut rings around their necks.

Illustration 18. Taiwan, Botel Tobago, first half of the twentieth century.
Yami woman in a ceremonial dress.

The hat is carved from wood (another kind of woman's hat is made of coconut leaves). The earrings as well as the rectangular ornaments of the big necklace are produced of nautilus shells. The form of the earrings echoes that of the silver breast ornaments worn by the men (Ill. 19). It is a kind of cocoon called *obaobai.* The rectangylar, axe-shaped objects are considered to be talismans and are derived from a supernatural creature of the Yami mythology. The bracelet consists of a small bent silver plate bound round the arm by fibers or cords. The woman wears a *raka* round her neck which is a large breast ornament reaching almost down to her knees. It consists of at least five, but in most cases even more, strings of beads kept in regular intervals by horizontal rods of bone or wood. The major part of the beads consists of agates; some, however, are made of different color of glass.

Since a large number of beads is required for the *raka,* only rich women possess such a piece of jewelry. It is true that poorer women produce similar ornaments, but they use seeds of different plants instead of stone and glass.

The round disks on the woman's breast are also made of silver.

Illustration 19. Taiwan, Botel Tobago, first half of the twentieth century.
This woman wears almost the same ornaments as the woman in illustration 18, but instead of a hat she wears one of the various hair styles, here decorated with a headdress with buttons made of mother-of-pearl, seeds and small beads. Mainly young women wore this kind of jewelry.

Illustrations 20, 21. Taiwan, Botel Tobago, first half of the twentieth century.
Both men wear a ceremonial silver helmet called a *vuragat.* Silver plates are put together so that the helmet can be adapted to the size of the head. One hole is left open. Such a helmet expresses a high social status since it contains much silver. Thus, young men can never possess a *vuragat.* The man in illustration 21 is also wearing silver bracelets and breast ornaments.

Illustration 22. Taiwan, early twentieth century.
An Atayal woman with tattoos on her face and an ornament of bamboo in her ear. There is a striking similarity between the motifs of the tattoos and those on the rod of bamboo. Only qualified weaver women were allowed to wear tattoos on their cheeks as illustrated here.

Illustration 23. Taiwan *c.* 1920.
A Paiwan man of high social rank wearing a headdress consisting of shells, leopard teeth and feathers. Several shell disks tied by a band are hanging over his shoulder. The man wears silver bracelets and a jacket of leopard fur. He holds a silver pipe in his hand.

Illustration 24. Philippines, North Luzon, 1912.
Only noble persons among the Ifugao population living in the region from Kiangan to North Luzon were allowed to wear the headdress illustrated. An important element is the reddish skull of the *calaos* — a hornbill which is a symbol for headhunt — between two horn-shaped wooden projections with feathers. Parts of the ornament are wrapped in a ceremonial cloth, hanging down over the headband. This headdress was inherited by the eldest son and worn only at special events such as the wedding of the owner or the *uhyga-uhy* ceremony, a very rare and expensive festival celebrated between the third and tenth year of matrimony in order to demonstrate the happiness of the family.

Illustration 25. Philippines, North Luzon, Ilongot, twentieth century.
A headdress for warriors, called *panglao,* which consists of the skull of a hornbill, fixed to a braided ribbon, decorated with beads and seed. Only warriors who had captured at least two heads were allowed to wear such an ornament. The braided backside is closely attached to the head, so that the whole protrudes and looks very impressive.

Illustration 26. Indonesia, Moluccas, 1940.
An old woman from Tinambar wearing filigree earrings made of gold, connected by a string of green glass beads.

Illustration 27. Indonesia, Sumatra, early twentieth century.
A young Karo Batak girl wearing a heavy silver earring called *padung.* The ornament is shaped like a double spiral, a form which is very common in Southeast Asia. One of the two earrings hangs down while the other if it is worn at all stands in an upright position next to the handkerchief. Frequently these heavy earrings are not fixed at the ear but at the shawl. In former days, when women still wore these ornaments in their ears, they were additionally fixed to the handkerchief to preve the ear from tearing. The girl illustrated only wears one earring. If both are worn, they are called *padung-padung.* Especially married women wear them in the way described above. S. Rodgers author of *Power and Gold* (Geneva 1985), reports that the way the earrings are worn symbolizes the ups and downs of matrimony.

Illustration 28. Indonesia, Bali, early twentieth century.
In contrast to the heavy pieces of jewelry of the Karo Batak woman the ornaments of this Bali woman are very light and fine. Like the Chinese aristocrats the woman lets the nails of her left hand grow as a sign that she does not belong to the working class.

Illustration 29. Indonesia, Kalimantan, early twentieth century.
Young Dayak people in festive decoration.
The girl wears a corset of rotan rings, wrapped with little copper rings, and decorated at the upper edge by silver coins and little colored beads. The protruding hair-slides indicate an influence which is not typical for Kalimantan.
The young man wears the decoration of a warrior which, however, is evident only by the sword and the tail-feathers of a hornbill. The bracelets made of shells, which have already been shown in illustration 14, are also frequently worn in Kalimantan. The remaining ornaments are for the most part of silver. There are obviously influences from the neighboring regions. Sometimes these ornaments are produced by Chinese smiths who are living in Kalimantan.

Illustration 30. Malaysia, Sarawak, before 1962.
An Iban Dayak plays a double-stringed guitar, called a *sape.* The Iban have been taught by the Kayan how to play this instrument which here is decorated with the head of a hornbill, a very common motif symbolizing headhunt. The way in which this head was used has already been demonstrated in connection with the Ifugao. This Iban man still wears long hair, more common in former days. The heavy earring is made of copper. Tattoos on neck, breast, arms, hands and thighs were very common for Iban men.

Illustration 31. Indonesia, Kalimantan/Malaysia, Sarawak.
An earring for men carved from the bill of a hornbill. The *Aso* motifs are described for illustration 32.

Illustration 32. Indonesia, Sarawak, *c.* 1960.
A Penan Dayak man, covered by tattoos all over his body. He wears an ornament of beads round his neck and a luxurious ear decoration. The teeth of a tiger can be recognized in the upper part of his ear, at the back of which are small beads. He wears heavy, massive copper rings in his earlobe; they are worn in different regions of Kalimantan and Sarawak. The form of these earrings derives from the *Aso* motif, a mythic creature, half-dragon, half-snake, with mouth agape. This motif is not only the basis for the design of the earrings but also for the different tattoos; the similarity between them is quite evident. The same motif can be found as well on other objects such as bamboo quivers, shields, wood carvings and beaded fabrics.
The combination of earrings and teeth or bones in the upper part of the ear is only typical for men, whereas copper earrings were also worn by women.

Illustration 33. Indonesia, Kalimantan, early twentieth century.
A Dayak dressed like a warrior. The wooden shield is painted with motifs similar to the tattoos in the previous illustrations. An important element of the warrior's clothing is the tail-feathers of a hornbill decorating the warrior's head as well as his back. These feathers cover the back of a leopard fur he is wearing. Moreover, he wears a very precious shell disk on his breast as well as shell bracelets.

Illustration 34. Indonesia, Kalimantan, early twentieth century.
This illustration clearly shows that Dayak women also wore heavy earrings or sometimes other heavy objects. The longer the earlobe is, the more it corresponds to the beauty ideal. The earlobes are pierced during childhood; as soon as the hole in the ear is big enough an earring with a diameter of three-quarters of an inch is put into it and later on further rings will be added regularly until the earrings reach down to the collarbone.
Exactly like the man in illustration 33, this woman is wearing

a necklace of beads around her neck with a rosette of beads in the middle. There are numerous rings of ivory round her tattooed forearms, together forming a pipe-like bracelet. The rings are imported from China. The hat is made from beads.

Illustration 35. Indonesia, Nias, early twentieth century.
An aristocrat belonging to the highest social class of this little island. The helmet as well as the moustache, earrings, an d motif necklace consist of pure gold alloyed with silver and tin. The tree on the helmet symbolizes the "cosmic tree," a symbol for the correlation and tension between everyday life and the supernatural.
The earring has the form of a double spiral and resembles the earring worn by the Karo Batak; here, however, earrings are worn by men as well as women. There are indications that originally men wore only one and women two earrings.

Illustration 36. Indonesia, Nias, nineteenth century.
A golden crown with five cosmic trees, worn by women of high social rank.

Illustration 37. Indonesia, Nias, early twentieth century.
Warrior from Nias with an iron helmet and a moustache. Hands, making repulsing gestures, are fixed at the ends of the moustache. These hands symbolize the physical resistance against mischief, and the symbols on the helmet, the magic resistance. The man wears a "warrior-band" round his neck, consisting of coconut rings and a copper clasp at its back. This is a characteristic ornament for men, a symbol of prestige and of success on the battlefield. This necklace is proof of the deeds of the one who wears it: he must at least have captured the head of one warrior of the enemy and brought it into his village. It is said that with this head he brings creativity and energy into the community. Moreover, after such a deed, a man was considered to be an adult and marriageable.

Illustrations 38, 39. Hainan, Ha-Li, 1937.
The Ha-Li woman lets her jewelry hang down only at festivities or ceremonies. A woman can wear up to fifty copper rings. As soon as the festivity or the ceremony is over, she binds the two bundles of rings together and wears them on her head (Ill. 39)

Illustration 40. Vietnam and South China, *c.* 1910.
Hmong (or Miao) woman wearing an indigo turban and dress as well as silver ornaments (see also Ill. 43). Large necklaces are very common in South China, Vietnam, Laos, Thailand and Burma.
The Hmong people originate in China. At first they were living in the regions of Kweichow and Hunan. Several centuries ago they moved to Yunnan and Kangsi Chuang and recently there have been migrations of nations again; the Hmong migrated to Vietnam, Laos, Thailand and Burma. Nowadays there also have been migrations, during the numerous wars in that part of the world.
The tufts of red wool over the breast recall the clothes of the Yao or Mien about whom we will talk next.

Illustration 41. Vietnam, Tonkin, *c.* 1930.
Mien or Yao woman. The Mien originate from China and now live in the whole highland of Farther India and in South China. The embroidery of the Mien women is among the most beautiful produced in the field. Girls are taught the

handwork from an age of five. Much time is devoted especially to the embroidery of trousers.
The jewelry illustrated is made of silver. The headdress consists of a wooden frame covered with an embroidered headkerchief. Fringes with beads are sewn to the headkerchief. This decoration was part of a wedding dress. The trousers worn by the woman in the picture are still common today. They are — at least in Thailand — still produced and worn, whereas the boots are very rare.

Illustration 42. Thailand, *c.* 1935.
Lisu woman with an enormous turban and colorful ankle-length garment. Over this she wears a vest, richly decorated with silver ornaments. Heavy solid silver necklaces, earrings, and bracelets show the wealth of her husband. The bracelets are engraved with geometric figures and flowers. Lisu use many geometric figures similar to the silver wire decorations of these bracelets, made by the Shan, a community in Burma.
Probably the first Lisu families went from Burma into Thailand around 1921. Today the women use more and more machine-made cotton or synthetic textiles.

Illustration 43. Laos, *c.* 1935.
Two women belonging to the Hmong-Deaw or White Miao (see also Ill. 40). They wear silver necklaces, earrings and big turbans. The dress of the woman on the left shows embroidered ribbons.

Illustration 44. Thailand, before 1963.
Young Lahu-Shi women dressed up for the New Year ceremony. The woman on the left wears typical Lahu-Shi clothes, whereas the other woman wears a festive dress showing Lisu influences, such as the fringes at the turban and the belt. This woman wears extraordinary beautiful silver ornaments on her back. Such ornaments are also worn on the breast; several tribes wear them, in different variations. The fish is a frequently used motif. The Hmong (Miao) and the Mien (Yao) mostly enamel these motifs. The bracelets of the woman on the left are similar to those in illustration 42. The round silver pins form the clasp of the jacket.

Illustration 45. Thailand, 1935.
A fifteen-year-old Lahu girl with a white turban. Here we can also see little silver globules on her jacket. The pins have already been shown in illustration 44. The girl is wearing an earring and silver necklace. The earring has the form of a spiral, as in Indonesia.

Illustration 46. Burma/Thailand, *c.* 1930.
A married Akha woman with her two daughters. The Akha originate from Yunnan in China, where most of them are still living today. The first Akha village in Thailand was built in 1903, near the border with Burma.
The woman in the middle is wearing the typical conical cap decorated by coins and similar objects (see also illustration 48). The girls wear little round caps also adorned with coins and beads. The girl on the left wears, additionally, a larger silver ornament on her cap which resembles those normally worn on jackets. Such an ornament is fixed also on her jacket and on that of her mother. The clothing is very typical and can easily be recognized: a skirt worn very low on her body and a bodice which goes down to the belly. This dress is also

richly decorated with colored stripes of fabric, coins, silver balls and cowrie shells. Over the dress a jacket is worn, with sleeves which are sometimes multicolored.

Illustration 47. Thailand, 1935.
A twenty-four-year-old Miao man with the traditional hairstyle and two silver necklaces.

Illustration 48. Thailand, *c.* 1920.
A young woman from Myang Payap. Although in *The Customs of Nations* (*c.* 1920) Buschan refers to a "Meo" woman, in my opinion, her headdress shows that she belongs to the Akha. Nowadays the headdress is much more magnificent and bigger than this one. The basis of the ornament is a broad headband adorned with small coins, silver buttons, beads and seed. On this headband there is a conical bamboo frame decorated with the same materials. Apparently another decorated frame has been fixed around the cone in this case. The whole ornament is finally adorned with feathers and cotton tassels.

Illustration 49. Burma, *c.* 1930.
Padaung girl in Pekon. The neck rings of the Padaung women are among the most peculiar ornaments.
From the age of five onward, new brass rings are put round the neck, so that a cylindrical form of metal develops, which stretches the neck. The forearms and the legs from the knees to the feet are surrounded by copper rings as well. Sometimes the women even put rings around their bellies.
It is said that men invented this as protection of the throat from tiger attack for women working in the fields or in the forest; for, such attacks could lead to the extinction of an entire tribe. Actually, these rings indicate beauty and wealth. The tribe owes its name to the ornament: *pa-daung* means "long necks." To take the rings off the woman's neck might cause her death, since the neck is no longer strong enough to support the head. If, however, a woman betrays her husband with another man, the husband may insist on taking off the rings as punishment.
The ear plugs with the little chains worn by the woman are made of silver.

Illustration 50. India/Burma, 1936–1939.
Ponyo Naga with the tattoos of a warrior. The two human figures tattooed on his breast show that he has already captured heads, so he enjoys great esteem. This man comes from the borderland between Burma and India. Motifs which first had been tattooed or painted on the body reappear later in clothing or jewelry. This becomes evident by taking a look first at the tattoos of the Ponyo Naga illustrated here and then at the clothing and ornaments of the Naga shown in illustration 51.

Illustration 51. India, 1960.
Nagas from the eastern district of Tuensang. The tattoos of the Naga shown in illustration 50 have been replaced by ornaments and cowrie shells. Although the human figures on the ornaments are almost identical with the tattoos they have only a decorative meaning here.
The brass pendants of the necklace were also a warrior's emblem. The war-helmets on their heads were worn all over the northeast and central east of the Naga country. These helmets are made of fine wickerwork, which is painted red and has a boar's tusk at each side. On the top of the helmet much

hair (possibly of a goat) and the feathers of the *caloo* are fixed. The *caloo,* a hornbill, is an important mythic bird for the Ifugao in the Philippines and for the Dayak in Kalimantan.
The man on the left is wearing a band with tiger claws around his jaw. The hilt of a short sword or a long knife, decorated with colored animal hair, can be seen over the shoulders of both men, on their backs. It is called *Dao* and is used for head-hunting as well as for everyday work.

Illustration 52. India, 1936–1939.
Filing, painting, and other deformations of the teeth are common customs in many parts of the world. In Africa teeth, like the eye teeth, are frequently extracted to distinguish tribesmen from neighboring tribes. As can be seen from the example of this Konyak Naga with his teeth painted black, deformations and paintings of the teeth are usual in many parts of Southeast Asia.
The man's helmet is completely covered with decoration of boar's tusks, bundles of colored goat hair, bundles of human hair and feathers of the hornbill.
The chieftain of the Longkhai, Mauwang, is dressed up for the war dance. His ears are covered by shell ornaments to which large bundles of yak hair, imported from Tibet, are fixed.
Mauwang is not only chieftain of the village and member of a highly esteemed family but also an artist; he works with wood and metal.

Illustration 53. India, 1936–1939.
A Konyak Naga with magnificent ear ornaments decorated with bundles of Yak hair.

Illustration 54. India, 1936–1939.
A Naga headhunter from Wakching with a headdress which is very similar to that of the Ifugao on the Philippines. Here again we have a combination of buffalo horns and the skull and feathers of the hornbill. Additionally, bundles of human hair are attached to the end of each buffalo horn. The ear decoration is of shells, and the necklace of boar's tusks. On his breast a brass pendant in the form of a little head hangs from a string of beads.
The tattoo is V-shaped, like that in illustration 57. This is the motif of the buffalo, sacred animal and a symbol for wealth.

Illustration 55. India, beginning of the twentieth century.
A Naga necklace made of copper, symbolizing the dignity of the head hunter; the motifs are two human heads and the spiral form occuring in many cultures all over the world.

Illustration 56. India, 1936–1939.
This Naga man, too, wears a fantastic headgear with especially striking buffalo horns. The whole ornament is adorned with goat hair, feathers of the hornbill and boar's tusks. The ornament is fixed by a band of tiger teeth. Around his neck the man is wearing the same copper necklace as in illustration 55. The bands decorated with cowrie shells hold the short sword which he is wearing on his back. The bracelets are made of ivory.

Illustration 57. India, 1936–1939.
Naga man, called Chingmak, head of Chingmei. The shell earring he wears shows an engraving with the same motif as that of the tattoo in illustration 50 and on the little jackets in illustration 51.

19

On his breast he has a tattoo with the buffalo motif, which is very similar to the motif of the double spiral used in other cultures.

Illustration 58. India, beginning of the twentieth century.
A pair of Naga bracelets made of bronze according to a method called *cire perdue*. These bracelets show the buffalo motif which can also be found in the tattoos in illustration 54 and 57.

Illustration 59. India, 1936–1939.
Recently married Angami Naga woman with long hair which signifies that she is marriageable and no longer a virgin. She wears skillfully manufactured strings, typical for the Angami Naga women. The big middle pieces are formed at the ends by longish carnelians. In between are eight strings fixed by sticks of bone. The strings consist of glass beads, carnelians and long white beads made of shells.

Illustration 60. India, Ao or Sema Naga, beginning of the twentieth century.
Necklace of shells and carnelians. The pointed pieces have been cut from a large shell.

Illustration 61. Sri Lanka, c. 1900.
Like women in India, Singhalese women frequently wear much silver and gold jewelry, often very fine. Gold-plated silver is very popular in Sri Lanka. Normally bracelets are worn in pairs, often decorated with filigree work. Several bands around the ankle are also worn and there are often little round bells attached to the ankle band hanging at the foot.

Illustration 62. India, c. 1920.
This elephant is from Udaipur. Elephants used for ceremony are decorated above their ears, on their foreheads, and between their eyes. They wear necklaces which extend to their front feet. The tusks are decorated and — important in connection with illustrations 61 and 63 — the animal wears bands with little bells around its ankle.

Illustration 63. India, c. 1900.
Silver foot decoration of a Tamil woman wearing three bands around her ankle. The upper one is made of overlapping silver wire, to create a kind of link effect. The band in the middle is hollow, with motifs chased into the silver; it has a screw cap and opens by hinges. The lower band, which has a screw cap as well, is made of heavy silver wire. The pieces interlock like links. At the bottom of the lower band several little bells are fixed. There is a ring on each toe but the big toe. They are definitely toe rings, much different from finger rings, although the same forms may be used. Similar toe rings are often produced from copper.

Illustration 64. India, early twentieth century.
This old woman from Himachal Pradesh (North India) does not wear her silver earrings in her ear but braids them into her hair.
She wears a stylish pin which is made of silver or copper. Here again the double spiral can be seen. The bracelets may be hollow or solid and produced of silver or copper.

Illustration 65. India, c. 1920.
Young Bhil woman with a headkerchief which can also be used as a veil. She wears a combination of earrings popular in India, which are actually pendants since they can also be fixed on the headkerchief or in the hair. A little chain connects the pendant with the ring in her nose, in this case a crescent-shaped ring in her nasal septum. Apart from strings of beads she also wears a silver necklace. Around her upper arms she wears little amulet quivers on red cotton, a very popular piece of jewelry. The one shown here is very simple, but often it is enameled or richly adorned with filigree work.

Illustration 66. India/Nepal, 1945.
Young woman with two different kinds of rings in her nose. One is through the wing of the nose — this is very popular in India — and the other is through her nasal septum. They may be made of silver, gold-plated silver or gold, and set with precious stones or glass.
Around her neck this woman wears a silver band. Such a necklace can be solid or hollow and, in that case, chased.

Illustration 67. Nepal, 1931.
A girl of the highest Buddhist caste in Nepal wearing golden jewelry. The Newar from Nepal are famous art smiths, and also produce Tibetan jewelry.

Illustration 68. Nepal, twentieth century.
Two ornaments typical of Nepal; a flower-shaped gold ornament, in the upper part of the ear, called *Karanphool,* and a large golden earring, or *cheptisoon,* in the lower part of the ear. For the sake of completeness a *dhungree* is worn in the wing of the nose.

Illustrations 69, 70. India, Ladakh, 1929.
Turquoise is very popular with the women from Ladakh and is used especially for their headdress, the *perak.* This consists of a long band of leather or felt which is covered with red cloth and reaches down from the forehead over the neck and the shoulder to the waist where it comes to a point. Apart from turquoise, agates and red corals are used as well for this kind of ornament. The form of the *perak* is derived from the snake, a symbol of the spiral. The combination of turquoise and the spiral motif makes the *perak* a symbol of immense power (see the Introduction). Next to the perak there is another ornament with many strings made of red coral beads, intended to represent the tail of a snake. The illustrated form of the perak with its numerous turquoises is worn by married women.
Illustration 69 shows the two ear-flaps produced of sheep wool, which are useful particularly in the cold climate of the Himalayas. The earrings and necklace contain many small beads.

Illustration 71. Pakistan, 1980.
In thre North of Pakistan, called the Hindu Kush, the Kalash live. The headdress of this tribe is as beautiful as the *perak* in illustrations 69 and 70. It is called *kapas* and reaches down from the forehead to the belt, too. Both ornaments may be similar in form, but the materials used are completely different. The *kapas* is made of woolen fabrics. The head part is decorated with 14 rows of cowrie shells, and a tassel, in most cases, of red wool, is attached to it. Under the rows of cowrie shells the *kapas* is set with shell rings and rows of little buttons, paillettes, beads and little bells.

Illustrations 72, 73 and 74. Tibet 1909, 1915, and 1950.
All these illustrations show the same kind of headdress. The drawings have been made after photographs taken by three experts in Tibetan culture. The illustration of the costume of 1909 is based on a photograph by Sven Hedin. Although this headdress is not decorated with beads it is, as are the rest, similar to other ornaments worn by aristocrats, who use the same motifs and forms as the other population. Only the value of the material used is different. The headdress illustrated consists of a bent branch which is put through a horizontal frame onto which the hair is fixed. The hair hangs down in plaits from its top. In illustration 73 an up-swept hairstyle is apparently worn. This aristocratic woman from the region of Tsang, wearing a festive dress, has been photographed by Alexandra David-Neel. Her jewelry partially resembles that in illustration 77.
Illustration 74 was drawn from a photograph by Heinrich Harrer, who proved his ability as a consultant in Lhasa and has even been ennobled. He mixed with the best society and described these people like nobody else. His photograph shows clearly how many turquoises, beads and large red corals such people wore on their heads.
Together with the fantastic hairstyles worn in Mongolia, this kind of headdress figures among the most extraordinary in the whole of Central Asia. This headdress can also be found with several little plaits, covered by red fabrics, running from the head to the edges of the frame and united to a thicker plait there.

Illustration 75. Tibet, 1956.
Woman from Lhasa with characteristic jewelry and head-dress for the central province of Ü. The hair hangs over a frame, which makes it look like two upright horns. Covered by red or blue cotton, the frame is set with strings of beads and enormous red coral. The necklace also consists of red coral.
Red coral is very popular in Tibet as well as in Mongolia and China, because red is the color of good luck. In Tibet the use of red has a long tradition. The orthodox monks completely dress in red and form the "red sect;" another group of monks belong to the "yellow sect."
Apart from red coral, turquoises, beads, jade and glass, *dzi* or *gsi* beads are used for the illustrated strings. *Dzi* or *gsi* is a precious variant of agate which only exists in the Himalayas. There are both round and long beads of this kind. Beside un-dulatory lines in dark brown or black, the long beads can also have rings or squares which are called *mig*, or "eyes." A *gsi* can have up to twelve eyes; stones with 9 eyes are the most precious due to their protective magic power. For Tibetans and other peoples from the Himalayas the *gsi* is a precious stone of supernatural origin, and is sold only unwillingly, because people believe this would attract misfortune like disease and death. The round *gsi* stones are even more precious than the long ones. A lot of *gsi* stones worn are copies made of glass, horn or ivory. The material is engraved three-quarters of an inch deep; lacquer is ground into the ridges and finally the whole stone is polished intensively. (In this connection see also illustrations 74, 78, 79, 87 and 91.) Comparable beads are the etched carnelian beads, painted with sodium carbonate; lines and circles are drawn and in the end the stones are heated. This technique was invented in the Indus Valley *c.* 2500 B.C.
The large ear pendants and the amuletcase belong together. Both of them are mainly set with turquoises. The amulet-case, called *gau,* can also be decorated with rubies, sapphires, emeralds, pearls and sometimes diamonds. In this case the jewelry is made of gold, but it can also be silver. The amulet-case may possibly contain parts of clothing, hair, nails,
ashes and similar objects of saints, little clay figures or *Tscha-Tscha,* sacred bands of silk with magical buttons called *süngdü.*

Illustration 76. Tibet, 1956.
A Tibetan married couple of high social status in traditional costume. Men holding an important position wear long earrings with turquoises.
The woman's striped apron is made of several stripes of woolen fabric, produced on a small loom. The front side is brushed and warped; the interior side keeps its original fleece and is therefore comfortably warm.

Illustration 77. Tibet, early twentieth century.
Young woman from the best society of Lhasa. The elements of the headdress are almost the same as those in illustration 75 although this woman wears beads and red coral in her hair. The belt is especially remarkable. It is made of gold and turquoise, and strings are attached to it. The main part of the belt, the clasp, resembles an amulet-case.
The structure of the big necklace can be seen distinctly. There is an ornament made of many strings of beads on the left side of her breast; in the middle of her breast a round ornament can be seen, set with almost the same stones as the amulet-case. The woman wears a red shawl around her shoulders.

Illustration 78. Tibet, 1924.
Another variant of Tibetan hairstyle can be seen here. The woman is wearing a long string of red coral and turquoises mounted in silver or gold. When Tibetan women had not enough of their own hair, they added false hair, sometimes imported from China.

Illustration 79. Tibet, before 1969.
The wife of the Prefect of Gyangtse wears the characteristic Tibetan cap, furred inside and covered with wonderful textiles outside.

Illustration 80. Tibet, *c.* 1900.
Amulet-case with its contents. It is made of silver and decorated with animal motifs, such as birds and deer with their heads turned around, a very common motif in Central Asia. The deer, the pair of birds, and the water are signs for a long life.
The amulet-case contains two woodcuts, folded into little packages containing prayers and similar things. These packages are wrapped up in differently colored wool threads as an additional protection against mischief.

Illustration 81. Tibet, before 1969.
Man belonging to the staff of the Prefect of Shigatse. The characteristic yellow hat and the long earring, which is always worn on the left side and consists of gold, turquoises and a pearl in the middle, demonstrate his important position. In his right ear he is wearing a turquoise and a bead put through the earlobe by a cord.

Illustration 82. Tibet, before 1969.
The Dzong-Pön, the Prefect of Shigatse, belongs to an old royal dynasty. His high official status is revealed, apart from the earring, by the way he wears his amulet-case in a knot on his head.

Illustration 83. Tibet, 1930.
This man from West China (Amnei Machin Mountains) wears a hair strand knotted on one side of his head. A amulet-case as well as a rosary can be recognized around his neck. The men living in this region often wear their coats thrown over one shoulder leaving the other shoulder uncovered. They do so, as soon as the weather becomes warm enough or when the sun is shining, for freedom of movement. The rosary worn by this man has 108 beads; 108 is a sacred number for Buddhists.

Illustration 84. Tibet, before 1969.
This simple decoration is an earring made of copper with a turquoise. Tibetans always wear at least one turquoise: the same applies to the earring. According to an old superstition, those who wear no earring will become a monkey in their next life.

Illustration 85. Tibet, before 1930.
A Tibetan woman from the prairie east of the lake Koko Nor. Like many nomad women she wears most of her jewelry, in this case large silver balls with coral and turquoises, on her back. There are many variants of this decoration indicating to which tribe the woman belongs; the material used shows wealth or status. As well as silver, turquoises and red coral, amber, ivory, coins and shells are used, among others. The adornments belong to the headdress of 108 plaits.

Illustration 86. Tibet, 1930.
This illustration shows the chieftain of the Butsang Ngolok and his wife, the daughter of the king of Ngawa.
The nomads, accustomed to hard living conditions, maintained the rhythm of life that had existed for their people for centuries. They traveled with the seasons and exchanged skins, wool, salt, and coral for tea, silk, and silver from China. Because of their many journeys their culture became a mixture of Central Asian, Chinese and Tibetan styles and motifs. The *Chupa,* the big jacket worn by the two people illustrated, was commonly worn, especially in the East and Northeast of Tibet, in West China, in Amdo and Kham (Qinghai). The jackets presented here are the Tibetan version of a long garment worn in many parts of Asia. Since the climate is rough in these regions and the nomads live in tents, fur is used often for their clothing. Apart from their clothes, the married couple in this illustration wears typical attributes and ornaments of East Tibet. The nomads had traditional weapons, like the beautifully decorated swords, as well as guns, to use against robbers and for hunting. The swords were often imported from China but the ornaments and the marvelously modeled scabbard are typical East Tibet handwork. The number of turquoises and coral on such a sword expressed the status of the owner. The sword was worn in the belt on the front side of the body. The best swords were produced in Kham and were expensive. The nomads always carries their swords with them and placed them under their pillow at night. The man in this illustration wears a cap made of polar-fox fur. His boots are leather, and partially of woolen fabric. The jacket is furred with sheepskin, and the borders are trimmed with otterskin. Around his neck the man wears a large rectangular amulet-case made of silver with turquoises, and on his belt, a little leather pouch with a firestone in it, decorated with copper or silver. The bottom of the pouch is lined with a strip of steel. When the firestone is struck against the strip it produces a spark.

The woman's hair is braided into 108 plaits and the rosary consists of the same number of beads; the canon of lamaism has 108 holy books. The plaits fall down over her shoulders to her waist and form broad bands on her back, part of which can be seen here. Silver, amber, shells, turquoises and coral are the most important materials for the decoration of these bands, as well as precious jewels, as on the *perak* of Ladakh in illustrations 69 and 70. The bands on her back have different widths. For insiders it is possible to discover tribal affiliation or area of origin from the width, color and decoration of these bands (Ill. 85).
Tibetan women always wear their plaits on the back, whereas the women from Mongolia, Tucheng and Uighur wear them on their breast. Married women part their hair in the middle of their head, in contrast to unmarried women. Moreover, married women wear more precious jewelry than unmarried women. Compared to nomad women the farmers' wives wear few plaits and sometimes even just one thick plait, extended with black hair, cords or bands.
As well as the headdress, a nomad woman wears jewelry around her neck and wrists, on her breast, in her ears, on her fingers and on her belt. Some earrings are smaller, some larger and sometimes they are made of pure silver or gold. They can become so heavy that they must be fixed above the ear in the hair by a little chain or leather band so that the ear does not get longer, or even tear (the Dajaks, in contrast, intend to make the ear longer).
The woman also wears a round silver amulet-case with a red coral in the middle. On her belt is a small leather band, decorated with an oval silver ornament which has a silver hook for the milk bucket. At festivities the hook is replaced by another ornament; in this case by a small amulet-case (see illustration 92).

Illustration 87. Tibet, first half of the twentieth century.
A twenty-year-old Mongolian woman belonging to the Kokot tribe from Tsaidam. The clothing and hairstyle are Tibetan, since she is married to a member of the Tibetan Hor tribe. Thus she is the daughter-in-law of an aristocratic woman, the "Queen Mother" of the mixed Mongolian-Tibetan tribes south of Huang Ho (the Yellow River). It is evident that this woman now belongs to an important family. Her jewelry made of silver, corals, turquoises and *Dzi* beads is very precious.

Illustration 88. Tibet, first half of the twentieth century.
A twenty-year-old man belonging to the Amdo farmers. His dress is trimmed with the skins of otters, leopards and sheep; his cap is furred with foxskin. Woolen threads are tied around his forehead in order to keep his hair upswept. He has only one heavy ring in his left ear. On his middle finger he wears a "saddle-ring." His sword is richly decorated (see illustration 86).

Illustration 89. Tibet, first half of the twentieth century.
A thirty-five-year-old Amdo farmer's wife from the south of

Koko Nor. On the upper left side of her silver amulet-case a ring can be seen, of the same kind as that of the young man in illustration 88. The pointed cap is often worn in these northern regions (see illustration 85).

Illustration 90. Tibet, first half of the twentieth century.
A nomad woman from Cham Ri with magnificent ornaments. The chased silver plate under the amulet-case is very beautiful. The motif on this plate, two dragons fighting for a pearl, is known in Tibet as well as in China and Mongolia; it was the emblem on an emperor's shield in China during the Han to Tj'ing dynasties, but it is also a frequently used motif for ornaments in Central Asia. It can be found in chased work on amulet-cases, as well as in embroidery. Bracelets with this motif have, for example, the head of a dragon at each end and a ball between. This motif is only one of a series of Chinese symbols, called "the eight preciousnesses." This piece of jewelry symbolizes the sun.

Illustration 91. Tibet, first half of the twentieth century.
A Mongolian woman from Tsaidam. Her plaits hang over her breast in the typical Mongolian way and are wrapped in cloth with large engraved silver ornaments. The upper ornaments represent the mystical knot, one of the eight Buddhist signs of good luck. The other seven signs are: the wheel of law, the cone shell, the umbrella, the canopy, the lotus flower, the vase and the fish.

Illustration 92. Tibet, first half of the twentieth century.
Woman from Amdo. On her belt we see the characteristic jewelry of a cattle-herding nomad woman. At its left she always wears a pendant with an oval ornament. The pendant ends in a hook which holds the milk-bucket. This ornament is a typical example of an article of daily use which has become a piece of jewelry. At festivities such an ornament is worn on the other side as well, for reasons of symmetry.

Illustration 93. Tibet, 1938.
This nomad woman wears three of the most frequently used types of amulet-cases. The two bigger ones are enameled with blue. The round cases, and other round pendants, possibly represent the wheel, one of the eight Buddhist signs for good luck (see illustration 91). The wheel plays an important role in Buddhism, explaining the existence of the universe. Sometimes the wheel is replaced by the symbol of the bell, or a small bell (see illustration 94).

Illustration 94. Mongolia, c. 1900.
This Mongolian amulet-case and ear ornaments are very similar to the jewelry of the Amdo illustrated in some of the previous illustrations. Small bells hang from the earrings. The symbolic meaning of these bells has already been mentioned in illustration 93; they ring softly with every movement, to frighten off evil spirits.
The silver amulet-case between the earrings is adorned with red coral, turquoises, malachites and ceramic beads. Its border is decorated with a motif of soldered wire containing six additional stones. Normally five cords should hang from the case, but one is missing. The ten upper beads are coral, agate, turquoise, glass and ceramic. Below these beads the cords are divided into two rows of small coral pieces, sometimes interrupted by turquoise and glass beads. At the ends are pear-shaped agates. The earrings are pure silver with two green ceramic stones and a red coral. The stones are surrounded by motifs enameled in blue. At the earring five big beads are fixed, connected with silver wire. The largest is dark-blue lapis lazuli; the others are amber, transparent glass and coral substitutes.
The beads are separated by silver leaf- or collar-shaped ornaments, either enameled in blue or adorned with turquoises or coral. The round silver case in the middle is enameled in blue, and has a green ceramic bead in its center. Small silver bells hang at the ends of the fine little strings of corals.

Illustration 95. Mongolia, 1936.
A woman from Ordos in Inner Mongolia. She wears a luxurious headdress, consisting of a headband with many bead rows and ornaments on its front and back (see illustration 96). Before the hair is put into the textile quivers it is wrapped with ornaments mainly composed of red coral and turquoise. The custom of wrapping plaits can be found throughout Mongolia. There are different ways to do this, but the result is always of special beauty.

Illustration 96. Mongolia, 1900.
Headdress of a woman from Ordos, consisting of a black cotton headband with two earflaps and a flap for the neck. On its front there are three rectangular silver ornaments adorned with filigree work and inlaid coral and turquoise. A net of coral with several turquoise and silver beads hangs on her forehead, as in illustration 95.
Small silver bells are attached to the ends of most of the strings. Furthermore six silver rosettes are fixed on the band, each surrounded by four circles of red coral. On the back a silver ornament is set with coral and turquoises, and the ornament itself is also surrounded by coral and turquoises. The flaps for ears and neck are decorated as well. Moreover, four other silver ornaments are fixed to the neck flap; the upper is enameled. The mounted stone in the middle of the large ornament at the bottom is a malachite. Several big stones hang at the lower border of the flap: agates, turquoises and a single coral in the middle.

Illustration 97. Mongolia, 1910–1914.
A Khalkha Mongolian farmer's wife from the region around Uliasta dressed for a celebration. Her hairstyle shows that she originates from Jasaktu Khanate, or Outer Mongolia.
This kind of hairstyle is so unusual that four drawings are devoted to it. The hairstyle and clothing of the married Khalkha women symbolizes the legendary origin of the Khalkha Mongolians.
According to history the cow which for the first time gave milk to a Khalkha Mongolian inspired his deep love for the nomadic way of life and life as a herdsman. To remember this story and to preserve the cow as a symbol of freedom the women had to wear their hair in a way that recalls a cow's horns. They also had to wear dresses with high shoulders similar to a cow's projecting withers.
The headdress has a very complicated structure, the basis of which is a helmet-shaped little cap of silver wire filigree with two earflaps (Ill. 99) and a neck flap. Most often the central motif is a stylized flower of coral and turquoises surrounded by ornate soldered tendrils. Two identical silver ornaments hang from the silver cap at the temples, a big one and a smaller one below it. In the exterior corner of the larger ornament and at the bottom of the smaller one long silver strings hang down, ending in leaf shaped ornaments.
On the headdress of the woman shown two other orna-

ments, large corals with a leaf-shaped ornament, are additionally fixed. The black hair is made to shine with linseed oil, butter or sheep fat, and pulled back from the middle of the head, so that the ears are free. On both sides of the neck flap the hair is combed out evenly. The "cow horns" are formed by these two strands. They are held together by about five hair-slides of silver or bamboo. The slide next to the neck flap is the biggest, and is sometimes shaped like a wing. The other smaller slides — three in Jasaktu Khanate — follow the bent line of the "cow horns." Finally, another fan-shaped slide forms the transition between the horns and the plaits. Although all slides may be decorated, the last is the most beautiful. Very often it has the same motifs as the little cap.

The plaits can be left uncovered, as here, but the hair style can be complimented even further. In wealthier families the plaits are put into circular covers (see illustration 99), covered with brocade of the finest Chinese silk. Three rows of coral and silver bands are fixed on it at regular intervals. Between them chased silver plates are attached. There is still enough space left so that the brocade can be seen. A strip of Chinese silk brocade, at least 27 inches long, is sewn on the bottom of the covers. In illustration 98 the quiver for the plaits has a flatter form than that in illustration 99, although the arrangement of the ornaments is identical.

For special events or for traveling a high, pointed hat which looks like a crown is worn above the little cap. This hat has a high, slightly projecting brim (Ills. 97, 99 and 100). The crown is an ornament in itself, in particular the top which is frequently decorated with a big coral or other stone. In illustration 100 we see the red fringe that hangs from the top of the crown. Theories about the origin of this kind of hairdress differ from those for the "cow-horns." For the nomads the sheep is also an important animal and motifs of sheep or sheep horns are often used; these ornaments could represent the horns of a wild sheep. According to a third theory, this hair style represents the wings of a mythic bird.

Illustration 98. Mongolia, 1910–1914.
Married Khalkha Mongolian woman without hat (for description see illustration 97).

Illustration 99. Mongolia, 1938.
Married Khalkha Mongolian woman in complete festive dress. Above the temples ornaments representing the head of a sheep with stylized horns can be recognized (see also description for illustration 97).

Illustration 100. Mongolia, 1920–1929.
Married Khalkha Mongolian woman from Tushiyetu Khanate; the origin can be deduced from the horizontal position of the horns. The hair-slides are possibly of bamboo, but can also be silver (see also description for illustration 97).

Illustration 101. Mongolia, 1936.
Woman with a headdress from Chahar and hair-slides from Kharchin, the two provinces in Inner Mongolia nearest to Peking. Therefore the number of slides shows Chinese influence. The hairdress with chains is typical for a married Chahar woman from the Aduchin region. Three big red corals are fixed on the black headband and more on its side flaps. Four little strings of beads hang down from the band, four of which have a red coral at their tip and one a turquoise. The long coral strings, interrupted by silver ornaments with the motif of the mystical knot, are about a yard long.

The hair is combed back and then divided into two plaits which first hang and then are swept up again until they lie close to the sides of the head. A net of red coral, interrupted by turquoises, covers the entire hair style. To this net, ear pendants are connected, linked on the breast by a chain of four coral strings. At each end is a butterfly ornament, fixed to the ear pendants. These pendants consist of many ornaments hanging down, one below the other; on these red coral surrounded by leaf and butterfly motifs is fixed, which in turn is connected to the upper side by short strings of malachites, turquoises or coral. Below the ornaments, three little chains with the same kind of beads end in open rings adorned with little beads. The numerous slides are made of silver with filigree, partially enameled. There are stylized flowers and butterflies, to which silver rungs are connected which sometimes have fringes of silk at their ends. Fine silver strings are fixed to these ornaments, in turn decorated with enameled butterfly-shaped ornaments. At the ends there are little strings which end on the shoulder in tiny leaf-shaped ornaments. The earrings are also adorned with these little chains.

Illustration 102. Mongolia, 1936.
Since this woman is wearing less jewelry, the net of coral, and the manner in which the ear pendants are attached to it, can be seen more clearly.

Illustration 103. Mongolia, 1933.
Woman from Chahar with a net of coral. This net is used only at ceremonies, when the complete hairdress is worn.

Illustration 104. Mongolia, 1910–1914.
When the Khalkha women were dressed in the traditional way, their power was symbolized by five elements of their costume: the upright hat brim, the two hoof-shaped cuffs at the sleeves, and the two upright points of the boots. It was believed that as long as this tradition existed, the Mongolians would remain an independent nation. A group of women dressed in this manner, galloping through the steppe, could easily be mistaken for a horde of well armed and helmet-wearing warriors. Such errors were reported as early as the Middle Ages.

Illustration 105. Siberia, c. 1900.
Buriatic woman from Transbaikalia, north of Mongolia, in a festive dress very similar to those from Mongolia. The amulets show clearly that these women had the same religion as their Tibetan and Mongolian sisters. Their clothes are made of Chinese silk, as are the cases used to cover their plaits. These are set with corals, turquoises or malachites.
At the top of the ears are epaulet-like ornaments. Into the plait a horizontally protruding frame is braided; the ornaments are arranged around this frame. The red coral is the main part of this ear decoration.

Illustration 106 and 108. China, 1870.
Front and back view of a Chinese woman with Manchurian hair style, common in the Ch'ing period between 1644 and 1912.
In particular the back view shows how the hair was arranged; however this is not the only way — even higher hair styles were worn. In any case, frames of steel wire and silver rods were used, around which the hair was arranged. On the top a long flat hair-slide with a flower pattern is fixed. At its end

butterflies are attached. This hair-slide is made of gold-plated silver. The butterflies are enameled or adorned with the blue wing or dorsal feathers of the kingfisher (*fei-ts'ui* in Chinese). During the Manchu period these feathers were employed above all for jewelry produced in Canton or Peking. The feathers are pasted directly on the background. The only argument against this ornament was the relatively short durability. The kingfisher originated in the South; the feathers came from Kwangsi Chuang, Annam, and Tonkin to North China.

At the ends of the winglike hair style of the woman one can see the small blue-enameled ornaments of the frame. Most of the hairpins are attached at the front of the hair style, in particular those with flower and butterfly motifs which recur in the earrings.

The butterfly, a frequently used motif in China and Mongolia (and elsewhere) stands for good luck and summer.

Illustration 107. China, seventeenth–eighteenth century.
Hair pin. The butterflies, leaves, flowers and Chinese letters are produced of gold-plated brass. The pin is made of silver. The Chinese letter means joy, good luck.

Illustration 109. China, nineteenth century.
Hairpin of copper, whose leaf-, flower-, and butterfly-shaped ornaments are covered with feathers of the kingfisher. In the middle a pearl is attached. The ornaments are connected to the hairpin by spirals. One of the spirals is worn out; it is not known, however, whether the hairpin was worn in this way or whether this happened afterward. The whole piece of jewelry is eight inches long, the hairpin, six inches.

Illustration 110. China, 1862–1863.
Chinese dignitary in civil service.
Under his jacket he is wearing the python garment for dignitaries. The dragon garment was worn only at court. His boots are made of black satin. The jacket shows the ornaments for civil servants. The species of bird indicates the rank. There are nine species of birds, a dragon with five heads for princes, and dogs, leopards and tigers for officers.

These ornaments were always square, except those for the relatives of the Emperor. Civilian dignitaries from the fourth rank and higher had to wear the official chain, which resembles the Buddhist rosary worn in Tibet. This is a good example of an originally religious piece of jewelry later only used as a status symbol.

Around his neck the man is wearing a collar covered with the same motifs as on his clothes. On his head he is wearing a summer hat. The jewel on his hat indicates, like the bird motif, a particular rank. Since the man has a red coral on his hat and a golden pheasant on his coat, he must belong to the second highest rank.

Illustration 111. Japan, 1909.
Ainu woman with a mouth tattoo. Similarly to the Maoris, these peoples used to have tattoos on and around the lips. In former times the Ainu probably populated a much larger cultural region, but in the recent past they settled only on Hokkaido, South Sachalin and the Kuril Islands. Today an estimated 12,000 Ainu live only on Hokkaido.

Only the Ainu women wore tattoos. The tattoo has a socio-religious significance; it must be finished before marriage and thus is connected with the marriageable age of the woman.

The ornaments on the clothes, which are the same for men and women, consist of accolade motifs put together. The earrings are made of brass, as well as the pendant. The biggest beads consist of metal (nickel) and were produced by the Ainu themselves. The colored glass beads come from Japan.

Illustration 112 and 115. Japan, c. 1900.
Like no other nation, the Japanese have illustrated their clothing and jewelry, especially the hair decoration. On numerous wood cuts the most fantastic hairstyles are revealed. The most beautiful kimono motifs are frequently shown clearly. The two Japanese women we see here show the front and side view of hairstyles common around 1900. As ornaments both combs and hair-slides were used. The combs were of tortoise-shell, ivory, glass or lacquered work. The hair-slides were made of the same materials or of silver, or decorated with textile flowers. From the beginning of the seventeenth century an upswept hairstyle was usual, and more and more combs and hair-slides of all possible forms and sizes were created to decorate the hair. This fashion continued until the beginning of the twentieth century. Today the girls wear the traditional hairstyle only on New Year's Day. Moreover, it is the common hairstyle for the geishas.

Illustration 113. Japan, woodcut, by Eishi, c. 1870.
114, 116 and 117. Japan, woodcuts, by Utamaro, c. 1800.
Four fragments of wood engravings by Eishi and Utamaro, clearly illustrating the use of combs and hair-slides.

Illustration 118. Central Asia, Kirgizia, 1932.
The Kirghiz women are wearing turbans. The fringes on the forehead, of red coral and mother-of-pearl buttons, show the kinship to the Chahar Mongolians. Much red coral can be found also in the long chains hanging from the earflaps of the head decoration. The silver ornaments in the pendants are worked in filigree technique and set with small corals and turquoises. The turban is covered with a headkerchief decorated with beads and fringes.

The Kirghiz live in the highlands of Central Asia east of Tashkent in the Soviet Union and in the farthest West of China, but they can also be found in the Pamir mountains in and near Afghanistan.

The jewelry is similar to that of Tadzhikistan.

Illustration 119. Central Asia/Soviet Union, before 1963.
Sarik Turkmen woman from the Soviet Union, near the Iranian and Afghan border, from Tachta-Bazar. She is wearing a *tumar,* a breast ornament made of silver, partially gold-plated and set with carnelians. The bands on which the ornament hangs are covered with small silver ornaments. The quiver in the middle can be opened and serves as an amulet-case.

Quiver-like amulet-cases can be found in many parts of the Islamic centural region. The Turkmen cultural region reaches from Northeast Iran and Northwest Afghanistan to Uzbekistan at the Aral Sea and Bukhara.

The Turkmen have numerous amulets and talismans to avert demons and the evil eye. They are worn mainly by women, young girls and children. Simple amulets are sewn on the cloth or on the cap. Many amulets, however, are pieces of jewelry of singular beauty. The *tumar* is such an example. In most cases this ornament has the form of a triangle. The carnelian is especially popular among the Turkmens. They be-

25

lieve that this precious stone protects from death and illness and brings the wearer good luck and peace. Turquoise is not as frequently used.

The Turkmen from the North and the Yomud at the Caspian Sea use — instead of carnelian or turquoise — glass of the same color. The Tekke Turkmen use glass very rarely. The materials employed are gold, silver and copper. The silver is partially gold-plated, leading to an especially good expression of the motifs. Beside flower and leaf motifs water, tree of life, mountain, butterfly and horn motifs are used.

The headdress of the woman shown here is covered completely by shawls.

Illustration 120. Central Asia, Iran, before 1978.
The small embroidered cap with a top of silver, called *gupba*, was worn by Turkmen girls until marriage. A girls aged 12 to 15 years, who was not engaged, wore feathers of the owl, the hawk, the pheasant or the cock on top of the cap. The *gupba* was decorated with coins, little round ornaments, small bells, fish-shaped ornaments and bead strings. After marriage the cap was replaced by the high hat for women. If, however, the dowry was not paid completely and the bride lived with her parents until it was paid, she wore her girl's cap during this time. Poor women sometimes wore the cap their entire life.

Illustration 121. Central Asia/Soviet Union, 1935.
The jewelry this Tekke Turkmen woman is wearing on a necklace has the form of a tree of life and is called *dagdan*. Dagdan means dawn or stands for the genesis of a new life of man. The blue beads in this piece symbolize the cosmos. On her head the woman is wearing the so-called *egme,* a slightly bent plate fixed at the front of the woman's cap, mostly covered by her veil.

Formerly the high headgear was woven from fibers; later it was produced of pasteboard, on which headkerchiefs were fixed.

This headdress is as monumental as the Turkmen carpets, which are known very well. It belongs to the bridal decoration and is worn by married women.

Illustration 122. Central Asia/Soviet Union, before 1963.
Tekke Turkmen woman wearing a necklace with one big and two small *dagdans* (see illustration 121).

Under the chin the *guljaka* can be seen, a pin for closing the dress or coat at the throat. This is worn daily and does not belong to the bridal decoration. Until *c.* 1920 this ornament was not worn by the Tekke. Originally it came from the Yomud who lived in an area reaching from the North of former Turkistan to Northeast Persia (today Iran), but later became popular all over Turkmenistan.

The headdress shown here is especially voluminous: under the big *egme* (see illustration 121) the *canne* is worn. The *canne* belongs to the group of *sinsile* ornaments. They are worn throughout Turkmenistan both by girls and women and have a very long tradition. In some areas they are worn only by unmarried girls and women, in other areas also by married women until the birth of the first or second child. Then only the *egme* is worn on the headdress.

Illustration 123. Central Asia Iran, before 1978.
Married Tekke Turkmen woman from Gonbad-e Kāvūs.
The type of headdress worn by married women can be seen clearly. The upper side is flat and wrapped in cloths.

The woman wears beautiful jewelry. A part of it, the *asyk*, a heart-shaped silver plate which is partially gold-plated, is covered with veils and normally not visible. These asyk are worn on the back and vary in length, sometimes a height of up to twelve inches and other times having a height of four to eight inches, as in the illustration. They belong to the ornaments hanging at or between two plaits. These asyk are a gift of the bridegroom's parents to the bride and she wears this jewelry for the first time at her wedding in the house of her husband.

Before marriage the girl's plaits may also hang on her breast. Instead of two plaits, she has frequently four plaits, two of which hang on her back and two on her breast. The jewelry is set with carnelians. The asyk take the shape of the female idols and are a fertility amulet. It may be that the spear form is also intended to avert the evil eye. The carnelian (stone of good luck) in the middle is doubtless the center piece, to which the surrounding objects are adjusted. The plaits are covered almost completely with coins and other small ornaments.

Illustration 124. Central Asia, nineteenth century.
Teke Turkmen ornament for the back, ten inches long, made of silver partially gold-plated and set with carnelians (see description, illustration 123).

Illustration 125. Central Asia/Soviet Union, twentieth century.
This Tekke Turkmen girl is wearing — as well as the *gupba* on her cap — the *čekelik* ornaments at both sides of her head. At the ear pendants there are hooks that can be fixed to the cap or the headdress. These ornaments are worn both by girls and by married women. The girl is wearing the *guljaka* (see illustration 122).

Illustration 126. Central Asia, Afghanistan, 1977.
During the first two months after marriage, the Turkmen woman wears the *chuba*, a veil covering her face completely.

Illustration 127. Central Asia/Soviet Union, twentieth century.
Veils or headkerchiefs are richly decorated with embroidery, small beads, coins and silver ornaments. The clothes of this Turkmen woman consist of traditional textiles as well as modern cotton cloth printed with a flower pattern and imported from another part of the Soviet Union. The three rows of round silver ornaments and the *capraz* right at the bottom are sewn on a black strip of cotton located at both sides of the headkerchief. Similar pieces are used also for women's coats; an example is shown in illustration 131. There, the ornaments are worn on the breast, at both sides of the jacket opening.

Illustration 128. Central Asia/Soviet Union, twentieth century.
Yomud Turkmen woman from Iskander in the Kadanžik region with the *guljaka* (see illustration 122) and an amulet-case (see illustration 119).

The process of partial gold-plating, characteristic for the Tekke, is not used by the Yomud. Instead, small gold-plated disks are soldered on the jewelry. The *tumar* on the breast contains only carnelians. The *guljaka* has only one carnelian in the middle. It is surrounded by twelve colored glass beads. In her ears the woman is wearing the *gulak chalka,* the earring of the Western Yomud, with soldered gold-plated disks and colored glass.

Illustration 129. Central Asia/Soviet Union, twentieth century.
Tekke Turkmen woman wearing a big *guljaka*, the *šepeli guljaka* (see illustration 122). The number of carnelians and ornaments have their own meaning. The jewelry is fixed to a red cotton cloth. Below the disk there are a series of pendants, each set with a carnelian. Since these ornaments are fixed onto the cloth, they retain their fan-shaped arrangement.
The circular form stands for the rotation of the world. The disk reflects the particular views of the Turkmen about outer space and the cycle of time. Space and time are symbolized by the arrangement of the carnelians and motifs on the disk. Several rows of silver disks sewn on the woman's clothes increase the monumentality of the Tekke Turkmen jewelry.

Illustration 130. Central Asia/Soviet Union, 1890.
This wife of the Khan, chieftain, of the Tekke, around 1890, is wearing especially precious jewelry. On the belly one can see the biggest ornament, the rhombic *gönžuk,* whose form resembles the *capraz* ornaments fixed in pairs on black bands (see illustration 127, 131).
At both sides of the *göɜˇuk* amulet cases are attached. On the right side is the triangle-shaped *tumar*, which has already been described. On the left hip there is the *doga-kumuš* or *cheikel,* a square amulet case. The term *cheikel* stands for picture or monument and means that the case contains little figurines of clay or wood. Both amulet cases hang on leather straps decorated with rhombic ornaments.
Around her neck the woman is wearing the *bukov,* a necklace consisting of a flat, more or less square ornament with pendants, that hangs on a ribbon around the neck. Moreover, she is also wearing jewelry on her forehead and ear pendants as in the previous illustrations. Around her wrists she wears the characteristic bracelets, the *bilezik*.
These bracelets vary in breadth and are worn in pairs. They are decorated with rows of carnelians. Most bracelets consist two rows, but even eight rows are possible. The longest bracelets can be up to eight inches long, reaching from the wrist to the elbow. In general, they are only worn at ceremonies, but women from rich families wear them every day. The bracelets are made of silver, partially gold-plated and set with carnelians. They are hollow so for reasons of stability are filled with a resin-like substance. The open ends are pointed.

Illustration 131. Central Asia/Iran, before 1978.
Here the traditional costume of the Turkmen woman can be seen distinctly: the embroidered trousers, the long dress with embroidered neckline, and the coat with the *capraz* ornaments on black cotton bands at both sides of the richly embroidered scarf, over the headdress. Around the headdress there is a piece of jewelry consisting of several parts, connected to each other by clasps.

Illusatration 132. Egypt, *c.* 1900.
Townswoman from Egypt wearing the *burko,* a veil. The obligatory veil is frequently so richly decorated that it itself is a piece of jewelry.
The ornament she wears around her neck is very common in the entire Arabian world. In most cases it is sewn on a cotton band.

Illustration 133. Ethiopia, before 1922.
The crescent-shaped earrings can be found in many parts of Northeast Africa. Beside the tight-fitting necklet the woman is also wearing a bead necklace, to which, as well as coins, a cross is attached, revealing that she belongs to the Coptic Church. A longer necklace partially visible here consists of a series of amulet quivers and small cases fixed by means of eyes to a wool cord.

Illustration 134. Palestine, 1925.
This young woman comes from Bethlehem. The most remarkable piece of jewelry she wears is the headgear, a kind of fez, the *shatweh*. This was worn also in the villages of Beit, Jala and Beit Sahur. It has a conical form and is made of linen or cotton with stuffing to ensure stability. It may also be made of pasteboard, covered by red felt and trimmed with cotton. At the top the hat has a thicker brim. In the nineteenth century the fez was sometimes crowned with a gold or silver disk. This headgear is decorated with gold and silver coins which belonged to the dowry and were also fixed to chains. If the *shatweh* is not decorated with coins, its fine embroidery can be seen. The majority of both the woven cloth and embroidery used for clothing were produced in Bethlehem.

Illustration 135. Syria, *c.* 1900.
Drusean woman with the *tantur,* a silver ornament with a height of about 18 inches, its lower part covered and fixed by a headkerchief.
The piece of jewelry, falling over the head and fixed around the headkerchief, is identical with that of the Egyptian woman in illustration 132 and is a common ornament. Around her neck and her arms, the woman is also wearing chains with coins.
At the evening of the wedding the bridegroom puts the *tantur* on the bride's head, which she must wear for the rest of her life. The *tantur* must not be made of silver; sometimes it was produced from tin or another less expensive alloy. This jewelry could be worn in different styles, with different ornaments, revealing the regional origin of the woman.
The bottom of the *tantur* was covered with cloths hanging over the back down to the feet and decorated with tassels. Over the *tantur* was the exterior veil, which was also very long. The Druse are an Islamic sect and live monogamously.

Illustration 136. Algeria, *c.* 1900.
Kabyle woman with fibulas (pins) and enameled jewelry on her forehead and around her neck.
A major part of the population of Maghrib — Morocco, Tunisia, and Algeria — are Berber belonging to the Mediterranean race. Whereas the fibulas have virtually disappeared, the old forms still exist in Maghrib. The most common form is triangular, which can be seen in several illustrations. However, as each tribe has different fibulas, there is an incredible variety of form. These pieces are often connected to each other by chains over the breast, which in turn may be very different. The Arab term for fibula is *khellala,* but the Berber have names for the pins in their own language; such as in Morocco, among others, it is *tisernas* and *tizerzai*.
The triangular shape is a symbol for the fair sex and fertility and can be traced back to ancient Mediterranean cultures. The next two illustrations show triangular fibulas. There are also other forms, like the round one the woman in this illustration is wearing, and both plant and animal motifs. The tortoise is a well-known example. In most cases the forms are

arranged in such a way as to show the number five, *chamsa,* the holy number. Thus the fibulas follow the example of the hand amulets and crosses, which also show the number five. Beside a practical (clothes pin) and aesthetic value, the fibulas fulfill also the function of an amulet.

Both the diadem and the neck ornament in the picture are characteristic for the Beni Yenni from Great Kabylia. These ornaments are enameled in green, dark blue and yellow and are set with red coral. Those who were not affluent used a substitute for the expensive coral — such as red celluloid — to benefit from the function of the red color (see introduction). The long beads are red corals; the striped ones are made of glass.

Illustration 137. Algeria, first half of the twentieth century.
Kabyle bride with enamelled jewelry of the Beni Yenni. The big round breast clip in the middle, the *tabzimt,* was in some regions a gift of the man to his wife at the birth of a son. The fibulas are triangular and are called *ibzemen.* Below the *tabzimt* there are amulet cases connected by a chain. Both the front and the rear side of the round ornament and the fibulas are ornamented, characteristic for the Beni Yenni.
The diadem, the *thaassabith,* is worn on the wedding day. The term *assabah,* from which the name is derived, means "bonds" (between the families).

Illustration 138. Algeria, c. 1900.
Woman of the Ouled Nail. The girls of this tribe went to certain cities to work as dancers and prostitutes. As experienced women, and with jewels earned by their work, they returned to their native villages, where they were sought after as wives. These women wore mostly the jewelry of the Aures Mountains, but also other jewels and many gold chains sewn on cotton bands or attached to silver chains. The beautiful diadem of pure silver links with motifs cut out, from which small chains with crescent-shaped ornaments hang, originates from the Aures, as do the fibulas.
The enameled ornaments on the forehead come from the Kabyles. They are round and fibula-like, the *tabzimt,* which are not used as pins here, but as a kind of diadem.

Illustration 139. Algeria, c. 1920.
Dancers of the Ouled Nail. Just as in illustration 138 they are girls who have lived temporarily as prostitutes. The bands with coins which are tied around the neck or the head can be seen very clearly. Both girls wear as well a great number of bracelets in pairs, since there is a great desire for symmetry even if a lot of jewelry is worn. The upper bracelet with the spikes is called *m'kias souar,* "nail bracelet," and was worn in Biskra and Bou Saada by the Ouled Nail. In the case of the open bracelet of the other girl the same technique as for the Aures ornaments in illustration 138 was applied.
The girl on the left is wearing ostrich feathers on her head. They have not only a decorative, but also a protective function.

Illustration 140, Sahara, c. 1950.
Tuareg girl from the Sahara, mixed with the dark race of former slaves. She is wearing different amulets in her plaits, silver earrings and a necklace of beads. The materials are manifold: glass beads and plastics, shells and silver. The shape of the little plastic ornaments is repeated in the square amulet of silver sheet, called *tereaut.* Just as in the case of the triangular fibulas the fertility sumbolism plays an important role here.

The pointed ornaments worn in this illustration are probably made of plastics, but originally they were produced of agate of all possible colors and were called *tanfouk.* Sometimes they were also made of silver, glass or stone.
The tringular form is not only a fertility symbol, but also a protection against the evil eye.

Illustration 141. Mauretania, early twentieth century.
Girl with a typical Mauretanian hairstyle, consisting of many small plaits, into which beads have been braided. On her forehead she is wearing a diadem of beads fixed to the plaits.

Illustration 142. Mauretania, early twentieth century.
Hartania woman, descended from the former black slaves. She is wearing beads threaded on small leather bands. On her head she has an amulet of silver sheet or copper.
In Mauretania many different beads are worn. Around her neck the woman is wearing a thin cord with the rosetta glass bead in the middle, called *šria* in Mauretania. The rosetta glass beads could be found in ancient Egypt, but it can be supposed that most glass beads of this kind worn in Africa come from Venice.
Amber is frequently worn all over West and Northwest Africa, both in necklaces and headdresses. Next to her left ear and at the beginning of the string of her right plait the woman is wearing a leather amulet. As well as the amber beads, beads made of carnelian were used for the necklace.

Illustration 143. Mauretania, early twentieth century.
This woman is wearing much jewelry: almost every plait is decorated with a small ornament or an amulet made of silver, gold-plated silver, beads or shells. On her head she wears beads of amber and a silver amulet. Into the plaits little shell ornaments are braided. In the middle of these ornaments a cross is cut out. Here, too, there are small triangular ornaments as in illustration 140. They are braided mainly into the plaits at the neck — they are a good protection against the evil eye and the back must be protected above all. The necklace consists of big amber beads with smaller beads between, made of wood or horn and set with silver wire.
In Mauretania and South Morocco the cross-shaped amulets are found frequently. They are produced entirely of metal and are then called *bogdad* or *mogdad.* They are manufactured of gold or silver as well as of silver-colored alloys or copper. The top of most of these hollow pieces of jewelry is covered with filigree work with small globules; the design may range from a cross to a star. The woman in the illustration is wearing a *bogdad* on a leather band and another one on a chain. The crosses symbolize the number five and thus have the same significance as the hand amulets existing all over North Africa and in the Middle East. Five is a magic number, generated by the center and the four points of the cross. This is a fertility amulet as well.
The amulet made of silver sheet on the woman's head is called *ktab el heggrab. Ktab* means book and refers to the content, an aphorism or verse from the Koran, or a magic number square, magic formulas written down by means of numbers. This kind of amulet is also called *gris-gris* and is known in other African countries by this name.

Illustration 144. Morocco, first half of twentieth century.
Bogdad from Goulimime, South Morocco.
About 50 years ago, these crosses were produced principally by Jewish smiths in South Morocco. There are several hy-

potheses about the symbolism. It is certain, however, that the number five is symbolic, like in countless other amulets. In illustration 143, 147 and 151 we shall examine that more closely. In connection with the cross, it refers to the four directions.

In most cases, the jewelry of town inhabitants in Morocco is very different from those of the farmers and nomads. Moreover, these is also another difference between the Arab population and the Berber. The drawings from Morocco show mainly Berber from the South of Morocco and Jews from the Sous and the oases of Dra, Dades and Todra as well as of the Tafilalt. In the large cities of Marrakech, Fès, Meknes, Salé, Tangier and Tétouan gold jewelry was produced among other things, but in the small villages in the South almost only silver or silver-plated copper was used. Only the Jewish women wore gold jewelry from time to time, but the style was similar to that of the Berber. The Jewish women also wore gold coins, or more frequently copper coins, since gold was too expensive. In former times the valleys of the Dades and the Todra were famous centers of mostly Jewish silver smiths. In particular in El Kélaa M'Gouna, and in Tinerhir the Jews were excellent smiths. When they left, the delicacy of the ornaments came to a standstill. The design and motifs became increasingly uniform, so the identity of the wearer was not as easily recognizable.

Illustration 145. Morocco, before 1980.
Haratin woman from the region of Djebel Bani, wearing much jewelry. Haratin is the same as Hartania (see illustration 142). The central element of the longest necklace is the amulet, called *l'herz*, occuring in this manner also in Timbuktu, which implies that the jewelry in these regions is more African than Arabian.
The amulet shown here hangs from a necklace, which is beautifully composed of amber, coral, silver and amazonite. The big pointed rings are only rarely worn as finger rings; primarily they are used as hair pendants. The rings frequently contain wool soaked in perfume as scents play an important role in jewelry in Maghrib.
The silver bracelets with the soldered globules can be found also in Mauretania, whereas the piece of jewelry in the middle of the forehead with the little pendants and the red glass is characteristic for the Anti-Atlas region. The big earring with the flexible disk comes from Africa.

Illustration 146. Niger Sahara, twentieth century.
Targui girl from the Aïr region. She wear heavy pure silver earrings. The Tuareg plait their hair very skilfully.
Around her neck the girl is wearing some *agades,* crosses made of pure silver, as they are worn by different Tuareg groups.

Illustration 147. Sahara, twentieth century.
Young Tuareg girl with a thin cord, in the middle of which a silver *in gall* cross with a red agate or red glass, as well as crosses of the type *tahoua* or *agades* of pure silver, are fixed. The *in gall* cross is also called *tanfouk n'azraf* and belongs to the ornament types shown in illustration 140. Those who want to know more about the origin of these motifs are recommended to consult the book *Bijoux et techniques du Sahara* by Jean Gabus, since this subject is beyond the scope of this book. It should be mentioned, however, that the fact that all ornaments of the Tuareg are geometric can be explained by their isolation. They are living in even greater

isolation than their Northern neighbors, the Berber of Maghrib, who — under the influence of the Arabs — also use tendrils (arabesques) and flower motifs (see the fibulas in illustration 160).

Illustration 148. Niger/Sahara, twentieth century.
Tuareg woman with heavy silver earrings and a leather amulet on a leather band around her neck, called *gris-gris.*
The pure silver earrings with trumpet-shaped ends are worn by the Aulliminden Tuareg; the bracelets and ankle bands are almost identical, but have heavy buds at both ends.

Illustration 149. Morocco, before 1980.
Ait Haddidu woman from the Atlas Mountains with an amber necklace. Between the stones silver disks and red pieces of felt have been fixed so that the stones are not damaged. The smaller necklaces consist of longish red corals.
The fibulas are quite simple, and the remaining ornaments are also not so refined as those in illustration 150. Nevertheless, the general view is quite impressive.
The eyebrows have been made longer artificially by soot and saffron. Like the necklace, this is not only decoration. The color of saffron and amber is yellow, the color of the sun, and thus protects from the *jnoun,* the beings of the underworld. Charcoal around the eyes and a soot spot on the nose are black, the color of bad omen. This is neutralized by the red color applied on the cheeks: here red honey was applied. Honey is "the saliva of the prophet."

Illustration 150. Morocco, 1930–1950.
Woman from Southwest Morocco, richly decorated with jewelry, all of which is silver and partially ornamented by means of the *niello* technique (see introduction).
In the Anti-Atlas and the neighboring regions this technique is practiced very often, but it can be found also in other regions of Morocco.
The diadem with the silver cones is above all characteristic for the Ait Ba Amran, from the Southwest. These cones show the same symbolic circle as the round amulets worn by the Ait Ba Amrane around the neck. The round ear pendants are also worn by Tamanart women in the Anti-Atlas. The hair is pulled through shell rings. The fibulas are typical for the Anti-Atlas and the Djebel Bani. (See also illustration 163 and 164.)

Illustration 151. Morocco, 1930–1950.
Although her clothes look different, this Jewish women from the Sous is wearing the same jewelry as the Berber women from this region (see illustrations 150, 163). This is not astonishing as the Jews were among the best smiths. The Jewish population living in the Sous and the Anti-Atlas had originally come from Spain. During the Spanish Inquisition many fled to Morocco, where they were forced to live in special quarters of the cities, the *mellah.* These quarters were outside the medina, the center of the cities. The exodus from Spain continued over a number of years and the *mellahs* became overcrowded, causing the refugees to migrate farther and farther along the Atlantic coast to Mogador (Essaouira), Safi and finally to Tiznit. They arrived also at the Anti-Atlas. They have maintained their traditions, so their clothing still resembles that worn in Spain in the sixteenth century.
The jewelry worn by this woman is, as in illustration 154, characteristic for the Sous region, and in particular for Tiznit. The large ball-shaped beads are especially typical. They

are green, decorated with enameled yellow circles arranged in rows. The other pieces of jewelry also show the characteristic green and yellow enamel.

The earrings are fixed by an additional chain, so that the red glass beads or garnets protrude. The chains consist, as well as the beads or smaller globules of the same kind, of red corals, coins, crosses, an amulet case and hand amulets, or *chamsa,* which means five. These, and variants of the chamsa motif, are, other than the fibulas, the traditional jewelry of North Africa.

In the religious symbolism of the Mediterranean peoples the hand has always had special significance. The Jews painted protecting hands on the walls and doors of their houses and wore hand-shaped pendants; they called them "the hand of God." The early Christians called their hand symbols "hand of the Virgin Mary," and the Muslims called them "hand of Fatima," the daughter of the prophet. In all three cases the hand is used similarly as an amulet. There are different kinds: the hand with the spread fingers is clearly the averting hand, the closed hand brings good luck. Hand amulets are often stylized, in some cases so extremely that the hand can no longer be recognized as such. Some pieces consist of five parts representing the five fingers. A well-known piece of jewelry is the *chamsa,* consisting of five circular parts and a middle ornament. Of course, there are also the crosses we have already mentioned (see illustration 143, 144).

Illustration 152. Morocco, first half of twentieth century.
Hand of Fatima with a salamander. The salamander crawls slowly but certainly toward the sun; in the same manner, the soul of man makes his way to God.
Salamanders are stuffed and hung in the house to avert evil spirits. The herb doctors sell finely powdered salamanders as medicine against all kinds of diseases.

Illustration 153. Morocco, nineteenth century.
Golden hand amulet from Meknès, set with precious stones. This is a typical piece of jewelry found in the cities, not geometric but decorated with arabesques in filigree technique. The difference between the jewelry worn in the cities and by the Berber population can be seen clearly here.

Illustration 154. Morocco, 1930–1950.
Jewish women from the Sous with the same kind of jewelry as in illustration 151. The eyecatching bracelets as well as the other ornaments have been manufactured in Tiznit.
An especially beautiful piece is the hat made of silver, already worn in illustration 151. Here, however, the veil is attached to the back of the head, so that the silver headdress can be seen more distinctly. The long, stick-shaped ornaments are enameled.

Illustration 155. Morocco, 1930–1950.
Jewish woman from the Dra valley. The clothes pins, or fibulas, can be recognized very distinctly here. Fibulas of this form come from the Aït Atta, from the Sarho and the Dra. The two fibulas are connected by a chain. The pear-shaped jewelry directly below the fibula shows a magic *chamsa* motif, a central square with four little circles. The necklace, too, consists of different *chamsa* amulets.
On her head the woman is wearing ornaments fixed by a net of silver chains. The ear pendants are composed of several bead strings. The bracelets are solid silver.

Illustration 156. Morocco, 1937–1939.
Young Jewish woman in her festive dress. Fibulas with coins can be found frequently. The fibula shown here is simple, but some of them are very refined. The ornament hanging at the headkerchief is derived from the earring.

Illustration 157. Morocco, 1937–1939.
Unmarried girl of the Aït Haddidu (Aït Brahim). Only after marriage may she wear a high headdress, against which the colored ribbons stand out very nicely (illustration 159). The fibulas have four pointed ends around the blue bead in the center. Thus it forms a stylized hand; moreover, the blue color protects from the evil eye. Fibulas of this type are also called "footprints of the jackal." The jackal is part of many Berber legends.

Illustration 158. Morocco, first half of the twentieth century.
Fibula made of engraved silver, from the central Atlas Mountains.

Illustration 159. Morocco, 1937–1939.
Married young woman of the Aït Haddidu (Aït Brahim), wearing her headkerchief in a pointed manner. On her head she has a conical quiver made of pasteboard or cloth, fixed with small plaits. Above that she wears the indigo veil. This headdress is called *aquilos.*
The tattoos on the woman's face show her region or tribe.

Illustration 160. Morocco, first half of the twentieth century.
Fibula made of engraved silver, from the High Atlas Mountains.

Illustration 161. Morocco, before 1980.
Berber girl from the middle Atlas with fibulas, hands of Fatima, a necklace braided with beads and a net of beads, coins and silver disks on her head.

Illustration 162. Morocco, *c.* 1930.
Berber woman from the middle Atlas. The jewelry she wears is worn by the Ait Youssi and Ait Seghrouchen in the Eastern Atlas. It is made of silver and manufactured by *niello* technique. The front part, on the forehead, has hinges. Seven little pendants are fixed to it. At the sides the chains lead upward, where they meet in the middle of the head and can be fixed to the headkerchief by a hook ornament.
The big necklace consists of three (horizontal) rows with five ornaments. Between the first two rows there are four rosettes. In the lower ornament row the hand form can be distinguished: the three middle fingers are at the bottom, the little finger and the thumb are on the sides.
The third piece of jewelry is composed of fibulas with a chain. Just like the other ornaments it is very beautiful. The round ornaments hanging from the fibulas are called ear pendants. They can be attached to the plaits at the top of the temples.
The great number of different geometric motifs applied, with the help of the *niello* technique, to the different ornaments is striking.

Illustration 163. Morocco, before 1952.
The Ida ou Kensous in the Anti-Atlas do not tattoo their faces, but paint them with yellow saffron as well as with red and black.
The smiths of this people were well known for their silver

jewelry, their daggers, and their powder horns. These pieces were set with garnets or red glass.

The fibulas here have a monumental form and surround a great number of small and big beads, coins and small ornaments.

Illustration 164. Morocco, first half of twentieth century.
Djebel Bani fibula with a triangular form very common for fibulas. This shape may perhaps go back to the Venus idols of the ancient Mediterranean cultures (see illustrations 140 and 147).

Illustration 165. Morocco, 1935.
Jewish woman from Tafilalt with upswept hair style, covered by cloths and an embroidered ribbon, resulting in a high, broad headdress.

Illustration 166. Morocco, beginning of the twentieth century.
Hand amulet made of gold-plated metal. In the middle *Allah* (God) is written. Around the circle in the middle of the hand another four hands form the number five; thus this is an amulet with double effect.

Illustration 167. Morocco, 1952.
Jewish woman from the Dades with a diadem of two coin rows sewn on a broad red textile band. Above it there is a chain composed of red coral, amazonite and enameled silver ornaments. At its lower border there are little crescent-shaped ornaments.

Illustration 168 and 169. Morocco, first half of twentieth century.
Two earrings with a pigeon motif in different designs: the left earring is abstract, the right is figurative. The latter earring shows clearly the Arabian influence. The first comes from the Dra valley.

Illustration 170. Morocco, 1935.
Jewish woman from Rabat; just like the woman in illustration 171 she is wearing quite different jewelry from that worn by the Jewish women from the oases in the South (see illustrations 151, 154, 155, 156, 165, 167). This woman is wearing a high headdress set with little pearls. Pearls were used everywhere in the large cities, both by Jewish and Arabian women (see illustration 171).

Illustration 171. Morocco, c. 1950.
Bridal decoration from Salé. The jewelry shown here is different from that of the previous pages. Its form and motif are Arabian. The diadem, or *taj,* is worn as bridal decoration, but married women also wear it at important events or ceremonies. The headdress consists of gold ornaments with semi precious stones, or "stones" of colored glass, surrounded by pearls. At the temples there are also strings of pearls hanging down that meet on the breast. The painting of the face is almost a continuation of this decoration of beads.

Illustration 172. Guinea-Bissau, Bissagos Islands, 1931. (then known as Portuguese Guinea).
Bidyogo man adorned with fringes of red and white wool, feathers, copper rings and shells.
Particularly striking are the hairstyles which still exist in some parts of Africa. The hair is cut completely to the scalp at some spots and, at others, short tufts, or hair circles, are left creating geometric forms. These are emphasized further by red or white coloring. In addition, this man from the coastal region of former Portuguese Guinea is wearing feathers on his head and fringes on his forehead. Such a headdress can still be found in particular among the Nuba and Dinka from Sudan as well as the Turkana and the Pokot from Kenya.

Illustration 173. Ivory Coast, before 1963.
Young girl with plaited headdress with cowrie shells and sisal fringes. Directly above the cowrie shells there are carved wooden horns whose tips are visible. She probably belongs to a dancing group of the "Société des jongleurs," performing the *sangnoulou,* acrobatic dances. This group has developed from the "Société du serpent," which performs dances in the region of the Dan, Wobé and Guéré. During the ceremonial preparation of the serum against snake-bites these young girls perform dances.
The painting of the face resembles that at the initiation ceremonies of girls, but on that occasion the entire body is painted with loam or earth colors.

Illustration 174 and 177. Zaire, 1930 and 1956 (then known as Congo).
Skull deformations are only possible in the case of newborn children — until the sixth month — while the skull is flexible. This is a very old tradition existing all over the world, but in recent times only in Melanesia and Zaire. The Mangbetu from the Northeast of Zaire shown in this illustration practice the wrapping method; the head of the child is wrapped with fibers forming a kind of close fitting cap. By this method the skull is lengthened and the forehead recedes.
The significance of this custom is unknown. The Mangbetu are by nature taller than their neighbors and perhaps want to emphasize their stature.

Illustration 175 and 176. Cameroon, before 1969.
Front and side view of a Fali woman from Kangu. Here, as in the case of skull deformation, the head is given almost an entirely new form. By means of lip plugs the mouth is pulled forward, even more emphasized by the three scar tattoos in the corners of the mouth. The arrangement of the remaining tattoos in the middle above the forehead show, together with the decoration of ear and nose as well as the little wool tassel, a certain sense of composition.
The nose decoration is made of metal or bones. For the lip plugs stone may be used as well. The ear decoration is worn at several points of the ear and consists of both metal and bones. A frequently used material is aluminum. The piercing of the openings in the face — of mouth, nose and ears — has a magic meaning. Holes decorated with ornaments prevent evil powers from entering the body through them. The deformations, in this case of the mouth, show moreover the affiliation to the tribe and the status of a person.

Illustration 178. Angola, 1932–1933.
Tyipungu woman with a big wooden hair-slide, shell ornaments, and a neck ornament of twisted fibers and beads, smeared with ocher and fat. The whole is arranged around the neck like a large collar and reaches up to the mouth.
This kind of neck decoration is particularly frequent in Southwest Africa, such as with the Ovahinga. It is similar to the jewelry of the Samburu and the Turkana in Kenya, although they use rings of colored beads.

Illustration 179. Angola, beginning of the twentieth century.
Hairpins of the Tyipungu women from Kapelongo, made of wood and bones.

Illustration 180. Sudan, early twentieth century.
Dinka woman wearing a great number of little metal earrings of copper or aluminum, a necklace of beads with small balls of bronze, and a plug in the upper lip.

Illustration 181. Central Africa/South Chad, 1938 (then known as French Equatorial Africa).
In particular the Sara women wore extremely large lip plugs. The piercing of the lips was practiced in many regions. In the Amazon region in South America, for example, this was common practice. Most lip plugs are made of wood. Looking at this picture, we can hardly understand that such a custom is based on an ideal of beauty. That is why it was believed at first that some peoples in Africa did this in order to deform themselves to protect themselves from slave traders. Although this may have been a reason in some regions, other reasons obviously exist as well, since this custom has been practiced in different parts of the world.
This woman is wearing film cases. Formerly she must have worn several rings in her ears.

Illustration 182. Zaire, 1910 (then known as Congo).
Wife of the subordinate king of the Bakongo dressed for dancing. The resemblance between the forms of the scar tattoos and the forms of the figures on the clothes is truly striking here. The wood engravings on many utility articles show the same motifs, as well as the beautifully woven mats.

Illustration 183. South Africa, 1898.
Zulu woman from Natal with bead necklaces and metal rings around her upper arm. On her breast she is wearing a square ornament made of beads. The pattern and above all the colors of these ornaments can be read, as it were, and play an important role in the relations between man and woman. By a certain arrangement of colors the girls and the wives convey their feelings of love or express their criticism to their lovers or husbands.

Illustration 184. South Africa, end of nineteenth century.
Basuto necklace with pendant made of beads, to which a small metal case with a relief picture of Queen Victoria of Great Britain is fixed.

Illustration 185. Niger, second half of the twentieth century.
Wodaabe or Bororo dressed for the *geerewol*, a dance in which the most beautiful young men of two tribes hold a beauty contest. The decoration is composed of small ornaments, chains, beads, shells, plastic parts and leather amulets. Traditional forms from the Sahara region together with different imported articles create a fantastic appearance. The face is painted with a mixture of red ocher and fat.
The winners are chosen by the most beautiful young girls. The festivities last seven days, with the ceremonies being held during the afternoon and throughout the night.

Illustration 186. Sudan, 1927.
Woman of the Aulad Hamid, an Islamic population group. On their heads and necks the women of this group wear jewelry of amber, silver amulets and silver beads as well as chains. The woman here is wearing small cowrie shells in her hair, too. The nose ring is made of gold.

Illustration 187. Sudan, 1927.
Headdress of the Aulad Hamid woman, rear view.
Just as in illustration 140 showing the girl from the Sahara, here it can be seen distinctly how different ornaments have been plaited into the hair. This kind of hair decoration exists in many parts of Africa, in almost innumerable variants.

Illustration 188. Brazil, 1817–1820.
Mundurucú with feather helmet and neck feathers. The Mundurucus have tattoos in long lines all over their bodies. The feather helmet consists of a cotton cloth, to which small parrot feathers are attached: at the temples strings of small red feathers hang, at the ends of which little black feathers are arranged in small brushes. Over the back long red-blue feathers hang, which also have little tufts of feathers at their ends. This adornment is called *akeri kaha*.

Illustration 189. Brazil, c. 1900.
Karaja with a diadem-like feather decoration fixed to the back of the head; the inner and outer circles consist of yellow-green feathers, and the middle part, of the feathers of birds of prey. The outward ara feathers are attached to the end of little rods covered with cotton. Apart from the ear ornaments (see also illustration 190) the man is wearing a long lip peg, common practice among the South American Indians.

Illustration 190. Brazil, c. 1960.
Karaja Indian with traditional body painting and an ear decoration of little feathers.

Illustration 191. Ecuador, c. 1900.
The Jivaro Indians live in the borderland of Peru and Ecuador and outnumber by far the tribes living more eastward in Peru, which in some cases consist of only several hundred members: there are still an estimated 50,000 Jivaro Indians. The man in this picture wears ear sticks. The woman has a long stick in her lower lip, formerly worn by all Jivaro women as a sign that they were of age.

Illustration 192. Brazil, 1955.
Tarirapé, Mato Grosso. Ear decoration made of wood, cotton, teeth and feathers, including also eagle and ara feathers.

Illustration 193. Brazil, before 1985.
From the region of the Juruena river, an Aripaktsa man with a nose ornament made of Macaw and Toucan feathers, a headdress of feathers and necklaces with teeth.

Illustration 194. Brazil, 1956.
Necklace of the Urubu-Kaapor with a bone pipe. The Urubu-Kaapor live at the Rio Gurupi. The ornament consists of cotton, plant fibers, and feathers; and the feather dress, of two little birds, and bones. It is a decoration for grown-up men. Smaller versions of this ornament, or copies, are worn by boys who receive them on the occasion of their initiation ceremony at which they are officially inducted into the tribe.

Illustration 195. Chile, early twentieth century.
Araucanian woman with a pin made of silver, used for

fastening the dress as well as the shawl. The pins are called *topu*, a term from Peru. They have a similar form as the pins worn by the women in Peru and Bolivia (see illustration 199). Besides the flat ornaments there are also ball-shaped ones, sometimes decorated by cross and hand motifs.

The *topu* were found in many Peruvian graves and were made of gold, copper or bronze. It is possible that the big metal disks were also used as mirrors.

In Chile Spanish coins particularly were used for jewelry. This was a custom practiced by many peoples in South and Middle America.

Illustration 196. Chile, early twentieth century.
Araucanian woman with large ear pendants, called *upul*. They are thin, almost square disks on a bent rod. They are manufactured from one piece of silver.

Illustration 197. Chile, nineteenth century.
Ball-shaped pin with pendant into which a dancing figure has been cut. Hands with spread fingers are fixed at the bottom of the pendant. The ornament is connected to the pin by a chain of red glass beads and small rods made of rolled silver sheet.

Illustration 198. Chile, nineteenth century.
Engraved silver pin from the Araucanians. In the center is a sun or a flower surrounded by flower or leaf motifs, to which four hemispheres have been fixed. The motifs were formed according to Spanish patterns.

Illustration 199. Bolivia, first half of the twentieth century.
Aymara woman from Bolivia, decorated for the *chola* or *metis* dance in La Paz. The belt with coins is a popular piece for dancing, since the jingling of the coins goes very well with the movements. On her breast as well as on her headband there are coins, too. The well-known, finely woven shawl is fixed with pins according to an old custom (see illustration 195). The small pins look like spoons. Frequently, they are made of Spanish spoons, since these have the same form as the traditional pins.

Illustration 200. Chile, first half of twentieth century.
Young Araucanian woman. She is wearing a *topu* with a little cross, which fixes her shawl. Above it there is a pendant of two small silver plates connected by link chains. On the upper silver plate birds are engraved, and two small hands with spread fingers are attached. Around her head, the woman is wearing two chains with little coin-shaped disks.

Illustration 201. Chile, nineteenth century.
Araucanian silver cross adorned with small human figures.

Illustration 202. Chile, late nineteenth century.
Richly ornamented woman with large *topu* pins, necklace and big ear pendants of the same kind as in illustration 196.

Illustration 203. Panama, *c.* 1955.
Cuna woman with golden ear decoration and a nose ring. Following a beauty ideal, a long black line is painted on the nose in order to lengthen it optically. Around her arms the woman wears strings of beads as well as closely fitting bands made of cotton threads. Her calfs are decorated in the same way (see illustration 191).
This decoration of the arms and legs is a widespread custom

among the South American Indians. Her beautiful blouse, called *mola*, is made by putting several layers of colored cloths one upon the other. Then designs are cut in and quilted, leading to a pattern which is rich in contrast. Today these clothes are an important export good. The geometric motifs go back to the designs which formerly were painted on the body.

Illustration 204. Mexico, 1964.
Zapotecan woman from Choapan in the state of Oaxaca with the characteristic headkerchief as well as a pair of very old silver hairpins, called *clavos*.

Illustration 205. Guatemala, 1936.
Guatemala's embroidered clothes are considered by many to be its most beautiful decorative art. Each region and village has its own special motifs and color combinations.
Another characteristic of this country's dress is the large cloths worn on the head, either in a pleated form or as a turban. The necklace of the woman in the picture is composed of Spanish coins and beads.

Illustration 206. Mexico, 1941.
Zapotecan girl from Choapan, Oaxaca, with very ancient jewels. Below them are medallions and two triple crosses. Her blouse, called *huipil*, is woven of very fine white cotton in a fine pattern.

Illustration 207 and 208. Mexico, nineteenth century.
Illustration 209. Chile, nineteenth century.
Two silver triple crosses of the Zapotecs from Oaxaca, Mexico, and an Araucanian silver cross from Chile, which greatly resembles the Mexican crosses. This is not astonishing, since Spanish influences could be observed in both countries (see illustration 236, La Alberca, Spain).

Illustration 210. Mexico, 1940.
Zoque woman, dressed for going to church, wearing a finely woven blouse, or *huipil*, and headgear, *tapar*, of the same fabric.
Around her neck she wears necklaces made of coral and gold, with a cross hanging from the largest. This necklace is very similar to the rosary and was widespread about one hundred years ago.

Illustration 211 and 212. Mexico, nineteenth century.
Two silver triple crosses of the Zapotecs.

Illustration 213. United States, 1874.
Although the Navajos have produced jewelry only since the middle of the nineteenth century, this "Southwest Indian" jewelry has become the most comprehensive production of Indian jewelry in the United States. Around 1900 it developed into a souvenir trade for tourists.
The woman shown here wears, as well as a turquoise necklace, a *concha* belt. *Concha* is the term for the round or oval silver disks fixed on the belt in regular spacings. These *conchas* come over Mexico from Spain, where they were used primarily as ornaments on horse bridles. They represent a kind of oyster-shell, an attribute of Saint Jacob the elder of Compostela ("Santiago de Compostela"), the patron saint of Spain.
The ornament is, among other things, a symbol for victory, and as such it has come to Mexico as an amulet. This is not

the only example; Mexico has influenced the Southwest Indian jewelry manufactured by Navajo, Zuni and Hopi Indians also in other respects. As well as Mexican influence, there were other influences from the areas east of the regions where these tribes lived.

Illustration 214. United States, 1880.
Fragment of a silver necklace, called a "pumpkin flower" necklace, since the pendants are believed to have been manufactured by taking the flowers of the pumpkin as a pattern. The motif, however, is derived from Spanish or Mexican pomegranate flowers (which represents a Catholic symbol for the unity of the church). The *naja,* the crescent-shaped pendant of the Navajos, has a rarer form here, with hands at its ends. It is possible that this hand motif goes back to the Arabs (hands of Fatima, see Morocco, illustrations 151, 152, 153, 166). It was possibly brought to the Navajos by the Spanish colonists. The Prairie Indians, however, use this motif, too; thus it could also come from them. Moreover, the hands are common in so many parts of the world, that one can also speak of a universal motif.

Illustration 215. United States, 1903–1911.
Hopi Indian from the Sichomovi village with a *naja* on a necklace of pumpkin flowers. In addition, he is wearing a leather band with United States Liberty-Head Dimes and several strings of beads made of shells and turquoises.

Illustration 216. United States, 1900–1920.
The clothes of this Umatilla girl from Oregon consist of deerskin with bead embroidery. This garment originates from the Prairie Indians, whereas the hat braided like a basket and the strings of beads made of shells are characteristic of the coastal regions along the Pacific Ocean. The earpendants are made of shells as well. The collar clasp is manufactured from the tail skin of the deer.

Illustration 217. United States, 1900–1920.
Shot-in-the-Hand, an Apsaroke. His tribe belonged to the Crow. He is wearing the leather clothes of the Prairie Indians, which are embroidered with beads.

Illustration 218. United States, 1900–1920.
Young Tolowa woman of Lake Earl in North California with a braided cap. Her plaits are wrapped in cloth. This hairstyle was widespread among the Indians in North America. It can also be compared to the covered plaits of different peoples in Central Asia and Siberia.
The ceremonial *yurok* garment of the woman is composed of two parts: a leather skirt reaching down to the ground, with strings of glass beads and different kinds of shells and, above that, an apron of the same material, falling over the side and back. The necklaces are also made of glass and shells.

Illustration 219. United States, 1929.
Red Cloud, a Sioux, in traditional clothes of leather and beads. Before European beads reached the Indians, they decorated their clothes with animal and plant materials. In particular the hollow spines of the porcupine were an important element. They were used both in their natural color and dyed. The spines, which may be five inches long, were flattened. Then they were threaded on buffalo tendons, in several rows, side by side. A similar method was used to fix beads on the leather clothes. It is called "lazy-stitch" technique.

Some five to ten beads are strung on a tightly stretched thread which is then fixed to the clothes. By this method several rows of beads were fixed side by side. Apart from this technique, beads were also used for ornaments and for weaving.

Illustration 220. United States, 1900.
The famous Nez Perce chieftain Joseph (called by his tribesmen Hinmatòwyalahtgit, "Thunder comes over the country") at the age of 61, with a feather headdress for war.
This impressive feather headdress which, in our view, belongs to the stereopyical picture of the "Indian," was actually reserved for few people. Only the most famous and courageous warriors were allowed to wear it. Each feather represented a courageous deed. Moreover, it was said to give the warrior strength and protect him.
In particular, eagle feathers and weasel furs were believed to have these qualities.
At first only the Prairie Indians wore this headdress, but later it was adopted by the neighboring tribes.

Illustration 221. Canada, *c.* 1900.
Kaw Claa, dressed for the Tlingit dance. In contrast to the motifs on the woollen shawl of the Chilkat from illustration 222, the embroidery on the breast shows French influence. This is evident in the flower patterns brought to the West some 150 years ago by Indians from the East who accompanied the Canadian furriers as guides or servants.
Around his head the man is wearing a diadem of grizzly claws. The nose ring is common in several tribes on the Northwest coast: the Haida and Kwakiutl as well as the Tlingit.

Illustration 222. Canada, *c.* 1900–1920.
Chieftain Anatlanash. He has a voluminous full beard, in contrast to the young men who pluck out their beard hair with tweezers. Around his shoulders he is wearing a woolen Chilkat shawl. The Chilkat learned from the Tsimshian how to treat the wool of the mountain goat. Despite the otherwise rather geometric and original motifs, the Chilkat branch of the Tlingit was retained on these woolen fabrics, in contrast to drawings on other materials. Whereas in illustration 221 the influences of other cultures are evident, the designs of this Chilkat "blanket" are traditional: they resemble the tattoos which can be found in particular on the breasts and forearms of important men and which portray heroic animal figures, representatives of their clans or their families.
On his head the man is wearing a wooden headdress, painted and set with abalone (ivory shell). The headdress is crowned by the beard hair of a sea lion and the sides and the back are trimmed with ermine. The motif consists of two heads of mythic birds: the hawk at the top and the eagle at the bottom.

Illustration 223. Greenland, 1906.
Inuit woman from East Greenland with upswept hair style, wearing a diadem made of beads; around her neck and on her clothes are also ornaments of beads. The ear decoration hangs over the ears. All the jewelry contains European glass beads.
The clothes in Greenland and in the north of Canada were made from the skins of seals, walruses and caribou. Moreover, the entrails of the seals and walruses were used, too; in particular, for the waterproof clothes of the fishermen, who had to sail out to the sea in their kayaks.

Illustration 224. Canada, 1924.
Iglulik-Inuit from Canada in festive dress. The clothes are made of caribou skin and wolf fur, partially painted, and decorated with many fringes of beads. Flower motifs of beads can be traced back to the influence of whalers and furriers.

Illustration 225. Greenland, 1930.
One of the most eyecatching pieces of jewelry of the Inuit of Greenland is the bead collar with geometric motifs and clear colors.
Although glass beads were not used originally — some of them came from Denmark — the Inuit had always had geometric motifs, formerly in particular for ritual adornments and tattoos.
The breeches are of white seal leather, adorned with flower and geometric motifs and decorated with fur at the edges.

Illustration 226. Alaska, 1880.
Man with lip plugs of ivory or bones. This kind of ornament was also made of jade or other stones. Jewelry worn under the upper lip, in the lips, or around the mouth can still be found today in various Indian tribes in South America, such as the Yanomamö, Kreen-akrore, Suya and Beicos de pau (Portuguese for "wooden-lip Indian"). They were highly esteemed. They can be found in African countries as well (see illustrations 175, 176, 180, 181).

Illustration 227. Alaska, 1900 –1920.
Whereas the men wore lip plugs, the Nunivak women had strings of beads under their lips which were pierced, too. The nasal septum is also pierced and a small ring with four glass beads hangs there. On the occasion of ceremonies or dances the women wear ear pendants with square pieces of ivory and colored bead strings.

Illustration 228. Rumania, before 1940.
Hungarian girl belonging to the Hungarian minority from Torotzko.
A characteristic feature is the red embroidery on the blouse and the crocheted collar borders. Part of the jewelry is functional, like the clasp of the belt. On her head the girl is wearing a kind of crown or cap of little pearls called *pàrta;* several rows of silk ribbons, on which flowers are embroidered, are hanging over her shoulders and back.

Illustration 229 and 230. Russia, *c.* 1900.
The wealthy Russian farmers' wives also wore bead crowns, like the Hungarian girl in illustration 228, but there were numerous variants. Two of them are shown here, one of Novgorod (illustration 229) and another of Vladimir (illustration 230). As well as the headdress cuffs, necklaces and ear pendants were produced of beads, too. Both women are married, since the hair of girls and unmarried women was visible under the headdress. The foreheads of these women are covered with fringes. These headdresses, *kokochniks, kikas,* or *povoiniks* could be found as diadems or with a closed crown. They could be quite extravagant, even if they were worn by farmers' wives, and were composed of gold brocade, damask, or velvet, with gold embroidery. Sometimes they were set with real pearls and precious stones.
Pearls were found in the large rivers and lakes in the north. Mother-of-pearl was very popular, too, and, in some villages, colored glass among the poorer population.

Illustration 231. Greece, *c.* 1920.
Macedonian woman with much gold brocade in her clothes. She wears a belt with a heavy clasp of silver or a silver alloy. Such big round clasps can be found in many parts of the Balkans, in particular in Bulgaria.

Illustration 232. Greece, nineteenth century.
Golden or gold-plated clasp for a waistcoat or jacket, with a double eagle motif.

Illustration 233. Greece, 1937–1940.
Young woman from Keratéa in Attica with bridal decoration. On her head she is wearing the *koróna* or *kselitse,* a gift of the bridegroom. In former times this piece of jewelry was fixed on the fez (see illustration 134). It is embroidered with golden threads and set with beads, little stones, glass and similar objects. On the lower edge Turkish coins are attached. All ornaments are fixed on woolen or cotton cloth, supported by a piece of pasteboard, so that the whole can be worn like a crown on the head. Around her neck the woman is wearing the golden *jordani,* and on her breast the *korthoni,* composed of several chains with coins. In the middle round ornaments are seen, called *golfi.* The gold embroidery on the sleeve is, like other elements, characteristic for the Greek wedding dress.
The Turkish influence can be seen very clearly here, which is distinct in many parts of the Balkans.

Illustration 234. Rumania, before 1940.
Saxon wife from Sibiu. The Saxons have been living as German settlers in this region in Northwest Rumania from as early as the twelfth century. Since this time they have had close relations to other groups there, particularly because their craftsmen were very skillful and distinguished themselves by the production of belts and furs. They produced them also for the Rumanians and the Hungarians. Nevertheless, the Saxons have retained different ancient customs, as can be seen in their traditional costumes. The gold-plated breast ornament made of silver resembles jewelry in the countries of the Baltic Sea as well as the belt clasps in the Balkan countries.
The remaining jewelry is also of gold-plated silver. Characteristic features are flower motifs in the embroideries.

Illustration 235. Bulgaria, before 1940.
From the region around Ruse a Bulgarian farmer's wife wears jewelry on her head, around her neck, and on her breast, mostly of small silver disks and coins. The jewelry on her head is almost identical to that worn on her breast, so that it can be supposed that the doves of the middle ornament can be found also on her head.

Illustration 236. Spain, early twentieth century.
Woman from La Alberca, a village southwest of Salamanca, wearing precious jewels, a major part of which is of Islamic origin. In between there are Christian ornaments, such as medallions, medals, amulets and crosses, called *rosarios.* Some of them are triple crosses (see illustrations 206 –212). In particular the big golden beads with filigree work — ball-shaped as well as cylindrical — very much resemble the ancient jewels produced by Jewish smiths in Moroccan cities, including Fès, Salé and Tétouan. They could be prayer quivers. Next to them the woman is wearing different medals dedicated to the Virgin Mary or other saints.

On her head she is wearing a headkerchief, with which she can cover her face partially. It consists of fine lace with silk ornaments.

Illustration 237. Spain, early twentieth century.
Woman from Ibiza in festive dress with the characteristic little Spanish drum. Below the gold chains reaching from one shoulder over the breasts, ornaments are fixed, including among other objects a figurative cross and an amulet with the picture of a saint.

Illustration 238. Germany, before 1940.
Farmer's wife from Probsteirhagen, Shaumburg-Lippe, in festive dress. Here, like in many other cultures, the hat was reserved for married women. The Germans have the expression *Unter die Haube kommen* ("come under the bonnet"), which today simply translates "get married," but refers to former times when a hat was placed the bride's head on her wedding day (see also illustrations 121, 122, 123 and 135).
The silver pin (resembling that in illustration 239, but not so large) is octagonal, and has different motifs. The necklace also contains a silver ornament, this time a square one, just like the clasp of the necklace. Both ornaments are decorated with pairs of doves as a motif, which is also used in Bulgaria (illustration 235) and on Moroccan earrings (illustrations 168 and 169). Other motifs are the date and a monogram. The necklace consists moreover of two square ornaments embroidered with beads as well as of large polished amber beads.
Amber comes from the Baltic Sea; in former times it might have had the same magic meaning here as for the Berber in North Africa.

Illustration 239. Estonia, 1931.
This woman wears the round silver ornament which originally was used as a pin employed to fasten the garment over the shoulders. At that time, however, the pin was not as big. Whan people began to wear the pin only as jewelry on the breast, it was made larger. In illustration 234 such a round pendant can be found, too. The motif of the double eagle can also be seen on the clasp in illustration 232.

Illustration 240. Netherlands, 1981.
Although Protestants and Catholics on South Beveland wear much the same traditional costumes, there are distinct differences. The hat of the Protestant woman is oval, that of the Catholic woman, square. The coral necklaces lie loosely around the neck of the Protestant woman, whereas they are close to the neck of the Catholic woman. Finally, the golden parts of the ear decoration are attached at the top of the temples of the Protestant woman, whereas they are higher in the case of the Catholic woman. The golden parts are the ends of a crescent-shaped silver clip . The coral necklaces end in a golden clasp at the neck. Under the upper cap is the *tipmuts* with a crescent-shaped hole, so that the big hair quiff, the *bles,* has place.

Illustration 241. Netherlands, nineteenth century.
Fragment of a necklace of red corals with a golden "spine clasp" in filigree technique from Laren, North Holland.
In contrast to the woman from Zeeland in illustration 240, who is wearing the clasp of her coral necklace at the neck, such clasps are worn under the chin in most regions of the Netherlands.

References

List of references to the colored illustrations, enumerated according to their sequence. The dates on the photographs correspond in most cases to their publishing date; thus the pictures may be older.

A. Collection Graham Foundation for Advanced Studies in the Fine Arts, Chicago.
B. Color photo, J. Scofield, 1962.
C. Collection Ethnologic Museum, Budapest.
D. Private Collection.
E. Private Collection.
F. Private Collection.
G. Private Collection.
H. Black-and-white photo, Boris de Rachewitz, 1964.
I. Color photo, Gao Jinli, Long Guanmao, 1985.
J. Private Collection.
K. Collection Ethnographic National Museum of Copenhagen; drawing by Inger Achton Dix.

1. Oil painting, Gottfried Lindauer, c. 1875.
2. Collection Otago Museum Dunedin, New Zealand.
3. Black-and-white photo, D. F. Thomson, 1947.
4. Collection National Museum of Victoria, Australia.
5. Black-and-white photo, Dr. H. Bernatzik, c. 1930–1935.
6, 7. Collection Auckland Museum, New Zealand.
8, 9. Black-and-white photo, G. Buschan, *Die Sitten der Völker*, c. 1920.
10. Collection Rautenstrauch-Joest Museum, Cologne.
11. Collection Otago Museum, Dunedin, New Zealand.
12. Color photo, E. T. Gilliard, 1953.
13. Collection Museum of Primitive Art, New York.
14. Black-and-white photo, G. Buschan, *Die Sitten der Völker*, c. 1920.
15. Black-and-white photo, Dr. H. Bernatzik, c. 1930–1935.
16, 17. Black-and-white photo, W. Furness, c. 1900.
18, 19, 20, 21. Black-and-white photo, Tadao Kano/Kokich Segawa, 1956.
22. Black-and-white photo, F. v. Reitzenstein, 1920.
23. Black-and-white photo, G. Buschan, *Die Sitten der Völker*, c. 1920.
24. Black-and-white photo, Worcester, 1912.
25. Collection Museum Barbier-Müller, Geneva.
26. Black-and-white photo, Drabbe, 1940.
27. Black-and-white photo, c. 1920.
28. Color photo, G. P. Lewis, c. 1920.
29. Black-and-white photo, G. Buschan, *Die Sitten der Völker*, c. 1920.
30. Black-and-white photo, H. Morrison, 1962.
31. Collection National Museum for Ethnology, Leiden.
32. Black-and-white photo, L. Chin, n.d.
33, 34. Black-and-white photo, G. Buschan, *Die Sitten der Völker*, c. 1920.
35. Black-and-white photo, P. Wirz, 1929.
36. Collection Museum Barbier-Müller, Geneva.
37. Black-and-white photo, Tropical Museum, Amsterdam, c. 1940.
38, 39. Black-and-white photo, L. Clark, 1937.
40. Black-and-white photo, Aymard, 1916.
41. Black-and-white photo, A. Sarraut, 1935.
42. Black-and-white photo, Dr. H. Bernatzik, c. 1930–1935.
43. Black-and-white photo, A. Sarraut, 1935.
44. Black-and-white photo, Boon Chey Srisavasdi, 1963.
45. Black-and-white photo, Dr. H. Bernatzik, c. 1930–1935.
46. Black-and-white photo, A. Sarraut, 1935.
47. Black-and-white photo, Dr. H. Bernatzik, c. 1930–1935.
48. Black-and-white photo, K. Döring, 1923.
49. Black-and-white photo, M. Hürlimann, c. 1930.
50, 51, 52, 53, 54. Black-and-white photo, Chr. v. Fürer Haimendorf, 1939.
55. Collection Museum Barbier-Müller, Geneva.
56, 57. Black-and-white photo, Chr. v. Fürer Haimendorf, 1939.
58. Collection Museum Barbier-Müller, Geneva.
59. Black-and-white photo, Chr. v. Fürer Haimendorf, 1939.
60. Collection Museum Barbier-Müller, Geneva.
61. Black-and-white photo, A. v. Schweiger-Lerchenfeld, 1904.
62. Black-and-white photo, H. v. Glasenapp, 1925.
63. Black-and-white photo, A. v. Schweiger-Lerchenfeld, 1904.
64. Black-and-white photo, B. Berg, 1932.
65. Black-and-white photo, G. Buschan, *Die Sitten der Völker*, c. 1920.
66. Black-and-white photo, F. Sattler, 1945.
67. Black-and-white photo, A. K. Banerji, 1979.
68. Black-and-white photo, M. Hürlimann, c. 1930.
69. Black-and-white photo, W. Bosshard, 1929.
70. Color photo, R. Bedi, 1981.
71. Color photo, H. Nègre, 1980.
72. Black-and-white photo, S. Hedin, 1909.
73. Black-and-white photo, A. David-Neel, 1915.
74. Color photo, H. Harrer, c. 1950.
75, 76. Black-and-white photo, V. Sis, 1956.
77. Black-and-white photo, C. Bell, 1925.
78. Black-and-white photo, S. Singh, 1924.
79. Black-and-white photo, P. Mele, 1969.
80. Private Collection.
81, 82. Black-and-white photo, P. Mele, 1969.

83. Black-and-white photo, J. Rock, 1930.
84. Black-and-white photo, P. Mele, 1969.
85, 86. Black-and-white photo, J. Rock, 1930.
87, 88, 89, 90, 91, 92. Black-and-white photo, M. Hermanns, c. 1940.
93. Black-and-white photo, H. Koester, 1938.
94. Collection Ethnographic National Museum of Copenhagen.
95. Black-and-white photo, M. Bodenkamp, 1936.
96. Collection Ethnographic National Museum of Copenhagen.
97, 98. Black-and-white photo, H. Consten, 1919.
99. Black-and-white photo, H. Hasland Christensen, 1938.
100. Black-and-white photo, L. Forbath, 1936.
101, 102. Black-and-white photo, W. Bosshard, 1936.
103. Color photo, R. Chapman Andrews, 1933.
104. Black-and-white photo, H. Consten, 1919.
105. Black-and-white photo, P. Labbé, 1916.
106. Black-and-white photo, J. Thomson, 1870.
107. Collection Museé d'Ethnographie, Geneva.
108. Black-and-white photo, J. Thomson, 1870.
109. Collection National Museum for Ethnology, Leiden.
110. Black-and-white photo, M. Miller, 1862.
111. Black-and-white photo, T. Athol Joyce, 1909.
112. Black-and-white photo, C. de Rodt, 1904.
113. Wood engraving, Eishi, c. 1780.
114. Wood engraving, Utamaro, c. 1800.
115. Color photo, W. Browne, 1909.
116, 117. Wood engraving, Utamaro, c. 1800.
118. Black-and-white photo, M. O. Williams, 1932.
119. Black-and-white photo, Tolstov, 1963.
120. Black-and-white photo, M. Hürlimann, c. 1930.
121. Black-and-white photo, M. Khosrow Pir, 1978.
122. Black-and-white photo, Tolstov, 1963.
123. Black-and-white photo, M. Khosrow Pir, 1978.
124. Collection National Museum for Ethnology, Leiden.
125. Black-and-white photo, Tolstov, 1963.
126. Color photo, A. Stucki, 1977.
127. Color photo, O. Nahodil, 1962.
128. Black-and-white photo, Tolstov, 1963.
129. Black-and-white photo, O. Nahodil, 1962.
130. Black-and-white photo, c. 1890.
131. Color photo, M. Khosrow Pir, 1978.
132. Black-and-white photo, A. v. Schweiger-Lerchenfeld, 1904.
133. Black-and-white photo, C. Stratz, 1922.
134. Color photo, G. Courtellemont, 1925.
135. Black-and-white photo, Bonfils, 1900.
136. Black-and-white photo, c. 1900.
137. Black-and-white photo, E. Grange, 1951.
138. Black-and-white photo, c. 1900.
139. Black-and-white photo, Lehnert and Landrock, 1924.
140. Black-and-white photo, Lutkie, n.d.
141, 142, 143. Black-and-white photo, Gillier, 1934.
144. Private Collection.
145. Black-and-white photo, W. Othmar, 1981.
146. Color photo, R. Gardi, 1970.
147. Black-and-white photo, R. Gardi, 1970.
148. Color photo, V. Englebert, 1965.
149. Black-and-white photo, W. Othmar, 1981.
150, 151. Black-and-white photo, J. Besançenot, 1930/1950.
152. Private collection.
153. Collection Musée des Oudaïas, Rabat, Morocco.
154, 155. Black-and-white photo, J. Besançenot, 1930/1950.
156, 157. Black-and-white photo, J. Robichez, 1946.
158. Black-and-white photo, J. Besançenot, 1930/1950.
159. Black-and-white photo, J. Robichez, 1946.
160. Collection Dar Si Saïd Museum, Marrakech, Morocco.
161. Black-and-white photo, W. Othmar, 1981.
162. Black-and-white photo, F. Benoit, 1931.
163. Color photo, J. Besançenot, 1950.
164. Private Collection.
165. Black-and-white photo, J. Besançenot, 1930/1950.
166. Private Collection.
167. Black-and-white photo, M. Barde, 1952.
168, 169. Private Collection.
170. Black-and-white photo, J. Besançenot, 1930/1950.
171. Black-and-white photo, n.d.
172. Black-and-white photo, Dr. H. Bernatzik, c. 1930–1935.
173. Color photo, B. de Rachewiltz, 1963.
174. Black-and-white photo, Dr. H. Bernatzik, c. 1930–1935.
175, 176. Black-and-white photo, J. Gauthier, 1969.
177. Black-and-white photo, E. Verleyen, 1956.
178, 179. Black-and-white photo, Th. Delachaux, 1934.
180. Black-and-white photo, G. Buschan, *Die Sitten der Völker*, c. 1920.
181. Black-and-white photo, L. Thaw, 1938.
182. Watercolor painting, N. Hardy, 1910.
183. Black-and-white photo, 1898.
184. Collection National Museum for Ethnology, Leiden.
185. Color photo, D. Darbois, 1962.

186, 187. Black-and-white photo, Dr. H. Bernatzik, *c.* 1930–1935.
188. Lithograph, Spix-Martius, 1823.
189. Collection Museé d'Ethnographie, Geneva.
190. Color photo, H. Schultz *c.* 1960.
191. Black-and-white photo, R. Reschreiter, 1908.
192. Collection Museum of Ethnology, Basel.
193. Color photo, S. Wellington, n.d.
194. Collection Musée d'Ethnographie, Geneva.
195. Black-and-white photo, M. Gusinde, 1931.
196. Black-and-white photo, J. Ackermann, 1908.
197, 198. Collection Museum of Ethnology, Berlin.
199. Black-and-white photo, E. Ernalsteen, 1947.
200. Black-and-white photo, n.d.
201. Collection Museum of Ethnology, Berlin.
202. Engraving, E. Radzel, 1894.
203. Black-and-white photo, K. Severin, 1936.
204. Black-and-white photo, D. Cordy, 1940–1964.
205. Color photo, P. Høst, n.d.
206, 207, 208. Black-and-white photo, D. Cordy, 1940–1964.
209. Collection Museum of Ethnology, Berlin.
210. Black-and-white photo, D. Cordy, 1940–1964.
211, 212. Collection Caso de Pancho, San Diego, California.
213. Black-and-white photo, 1874.
214. Private Collection.

215. Black-and-white photo, Field Museum of Natural History, Chicago, 1903–1911.
216, 217, 218. Black-and-white photo, E. Curtis, 1900–1920.
219. Black-and-white photo, F. Reinhart, 1929.
220. Black-and-white photo, De Lancey Gill, 1900.
221. Black-and-white photo, Case and Draper, *c.* 1900.
222. Black-and-white photo, n.d.
223. Black-and-white photo, Arktisk Institut, Copenhagen, 1906.
224. Black-and-white photo, 1924.
225. Black-and-white photo, 1930.
226. Black-and-white photo, E. Nelson, 1880.
227. Black-and-white photo, E. Curtis, 1900–1920.
228. Black-and-white photo, H. Retzlaff, 1930–1940.
229, 230. Color photo, N. de Chabelskoy, 1912.
231. Color photo, L. Popoff, 1922.
232. Collection Benaki Museum, Athens.
233. Black-and-white photo, M. Hroussaki, 1937.
234. Black-and-white photo, H. Retzlaff, 1930–1940.
235. Black-and-white photo, I. Steinhoff, 1940.
236, 237. Black-and-white photo, J. Ortiz Echagüe, 1933.
238. Black-and-white photo, H. Retzlaff, 1930-1940.
239. Black-and-white photo, E. Lendvai-Dircksen, 1931.
240. Black-and-white photo, H. Boekhout, 1981.
241. Collection Netherlands Open-Air, Arnheim.

Bibliography

If all consulted books were listed, the bibliography would have been very lengthy indeed. Thus only the most important works have been chosen, with most emphasis on those books which are possibly still obtainable.

Al-Jadir, Saad. *Arab and Islamic Silver*. London: Stacey International, 1981.

Bachinger, Richard. *Die Hand, Schutz und Schmuck in Nord-Afrika*. Frankfurt: Galerie Exler, 1981.

Barbier, Jean Paul. *Art du Nagaland*. Geneva: Museum Barbier-Müller, 1982.

Beresneva, L. *The Decorative and Applied Art of Turkmenia*. Aurora, Leningrad 1976.

Besançenot, J. *Bijoux Arabes et berbères du Maroc*. Casablanca: Cigogne, 1953.

Biebuyck, Daniel P. and Nelly Van den Abbeele. *The Power of Headdresses*. Brussels: Tendi S.A., 1984.

Bhushan, Jamila Brij. *Indian Jewellery*. Bombay: Taraporevala, 1964.

Boujibar, Naima Khatib. *Bijoux et parures du Maroc*. Casablanca: Royal Air Maroc, 1974.

Boyer, Martha. *Mongol Jewelry*. Copenhagen: Gyldendaske Boghandel, Nordisk Forlag, 1952.

Brain, Robert. *The Decorated Body*. New York: Harper & Row, 1979.

Campbell, Margaret. *From the Hands of the Hills (Thailand)*. Hongkong: Media Transasia, 1978.

Camps-Fabrer, Henriette. *Les bijoux de Grands Kabylie Arts et Métiers graphiques*. Paris, 1970.

Champault, D. *La Main*. Paris: Musée de l'Homme, 1965.

Conn, Richard. *Robes of White Shell and Sunrise; Personal Decorative Arts of the Native American*. Denver: Denver Art Museum, 1974.

Cordry, Donald and Dorothy. *Mexican Indian Costumes*. Austin: University of Texas Press, 1968.

Creyaufmüller, Wolfgang. *Silberschmuck aus der Sahara*. Frankfurt: Exler-Galerie, 1982.

———. *Nomadenkultur in der West Sahara*.

Davis, Maryl. *Mexican Jewelry*. Texas: University of Texas Press, 1963.

Delarozière. *Les perles de Mauritanie*. Aix-en-Provence: Edisud, 1985.

Dubin, Lois Sherr. *The History of Beads*. New York: Harry N. Abrams, 1987.

Exler-Galerie. *Alter Silberschmuck aus dem Jemen*. Frankfurt, 1978.

Fisher, Angela. *Africa Adorned*. London: Collins, 1984.

Flint, Bert. *Forme et Symbole dans les Arts du Maroc*. Tanger: Tome I.E.M.I., 1973.

Frank, Larry. *Indian Silver Jewelry of the Southwest, 1868–1930*. Boston: New York Graphic Society, 1978.

Frehn, Beatrice and Thomas Krings. *Afrikanische Frisuren*. Cologne: Dumont, 1986.

Gabus, Jean. *Parures et bijoux dans le Monde*. Neuchâtel: Avanti Club, 1962.

———. *Arts et symboles au Sahara*. Neuchâtel: A la Baconnière, 1958.

———. *Sahara bijoux et techniques*. Neuchâtel: A la Baconnière, 1982.

Gardi, René. *Unter Afrikanischen Handwerkern*. Bern, 1969.

Gargouri-Sethom, Samira. *Le bijou traditionnel en Tunisie*. Aix-en-Provence: Édisud, 1986.

Gerlach, Martin. *Primitive and Folk Jewelry*. New York: Dover (reprinted edition 1906), 1971.

Hartmann, Günther. *Silberschmuck der Araukaner, Chile*. Berlin: Museum of Ethnology, 1974.

Hatzimichali, A. *The Greek Folk Costume*. Benaki Museum. Melissa, Athens.

Hawley, Ruth. *Omani Silver*. London and New York: Longman, 1978.

Hiler, Hilaire. *From Nudity to Raiment*. London: W. Foyle, 1926.

Hoffmann, E. and B. Treide. *Schmuck früher Kulturen und ferner Völker*. Leipzig, 1977.

Höpfner, Gerd and Gesine Haase. *Metallschmuck aus Indien*. Berlin: Museum of Ethnology, 1978.

Jacques-Meunié, Denise. *Bijoux et bijoutiers du Sud Marocain*. Paris: Cahiers des arts et techniques d'Afrique du Nord, 1960–1961.

Janata, Alfred. *Schmuck in Afghanistan*. Graz: Akademische Druck, 1981.

Jefferson, Louise E. *The Decorative Arts of Africa*. London: Collins, 1974.

Kalter, Johannes. *Schmuck aus Nord Afrika*. Stuttgart: Linden-Museum, 1976.

———. *Aus Steppe und Oase*. Stuttgart: Hansjörg Mayer, 1983.

Kano, Tadao and Segawa Kokichi. *The Yami*. Tokyo: Maruzen, 1956.

Kirk, Malcolm. *Man as Art in New Guinea*. New York: Viking Press, 1981.

Klever, Katrin und Ulrich. *Exotischer Schmuck*. Munich: Mosaik Verlag, 1977.

Knuf, Astrid und Joachim. *Amulette und Talismane*. Cologne: Dumont, 1984.

Kriss, Rudolf und Heinrich. *Volksglaube im Bereich des Islam. Vol. 2. Amulette, etc*. Wiesbaden: Harrassowitz, 1962.

Leuzinger, Elsy. *Wesen und Form des Schmuckes Afrikanischer Völker*. Zurich: Lang, 1950.

Lewis, Paul and Elaine. *Völker im Goldenen Dreieck*. Stuttgart: Hansjörg Mayer, 1984.

Lincoln, Louise. *Southwest Indian Silver from the Doneghy Collection*. Minneapolis: The Minneapolis Institute of Arts, 1982.

Marçais, Georges. *Les bijoux musulmans de l'Afrique du Nord*. Alger: Imprimerie officielle, 1958.

Meilach, Dona Z. *Ethnic Jewelry*. New York: Crown, 1981.

Moor, Maggie de, and Wilhelmina H. Kal, *Indonesische sieraden*. Amsterdam: Tropic Museum, 1983.

Muller-Lancet, Aviva and Dominique Champault *La vie juive au Maroc*. Jerusalem: Musée d'Israël, 1986.

Verarbeitung und Verwendung von Stein und Muschelschalen. Basel: Museum of Ethnology, 1962.

Tracht und Schmuck der Griechin. Basel: Museum of Ethnology, 1985.

Orchard, William. *Beads and Beadwork of the American Indian*. New York, 1975.

Olson, Eleanor. *Catalogue of the Tibetan Collection, Vol. 4*. Newark: Newark Museum, 1961.

Prokot, Inge and Joachim. *Schmuck aus Zentralasien*. Munich: Callwey Verlag, 1981.

Rodgers, Susan. *Power and Gold, Jewelry from Indonesia, Malaysia and the Philippines*. Geneva: Barbier-Müller Museum, 1985.

Ross, Heather C. *Bedouin Jewellery in Saudi Arabia*. London: Stacey, 1978.

Rudolph, Hermann. *Der Turkmenenschmuck*. Stuttgart: Hansjörg Mayer, 1984.

Sagay, Esi. *African Hairstyles*. London: Heinemann, 1983.

Schletzer, Dieter and Reindhold. *Alter Silberschmuck der Turkmenen*. Berlin: Reimer, 1984.

Schoepf, Daniel. *L'Art de la plume brésil*. Geneva: Musée d'Ethnographie, 1985.

Sieber, Roy. *African Textiles and Decorative Arts*. New York: Museum of Modern Art, 1972.

Skrobucha, Heinz. *Äthiopische Kreuze*. Greven: Eggenkamp, 1983.

Snejana Blagoeva. *Bulgarian Jewellery*. Sofia: Septemvri Publishing House, 1977.

Stillman, Yedida Kalfon. *Palestinian Costume and Jewelry*. Albuquerque: University of New Mexico Press, 1979.

Sugier, Clemence. *Bijoux Tunisiens*. Tunis: Cérès Productions, 1977.

Sijelmassi, Mohamed. *Les arts traditionnels, au Maroc*. Paris: Presses de l'Avenir graphique, 1974.

Tamzali, Wassyla. *Abzim. Parures et bijoux des femmes d'Algérie*. Paris, Alger: Dessain et Tolra, 1984.

Tilke, Max. *Kostümschnitte und Gewandformen*. Tübingen: Ernst Wasmuth, (fifth edition), 1973.

Van der Sleen, W. G. N. *A Handbook of Beads*. Liège: Musée du Verre, 1967.

Weihreter, Hans. *Schmuck aus dem Himalaya*. Graz: Akademische Druck und Verlagsanstalt, 1988.

Windisch, Graetz, Stephanie und Ghislaine zu. *Juwelen des Himalaya*. Luzern: Reich Verlag, 1981.

Zerries, Otto. *Unter Indianern Brasiliens*. Innsbruck: Pinguin Verlag, 1980.

Zhao Yuchi and Kuang Shizhao. *Clothings and Ornaments of China's Miao People*. Beijing: The Nationality Press, 1985.

1.
New Zealand

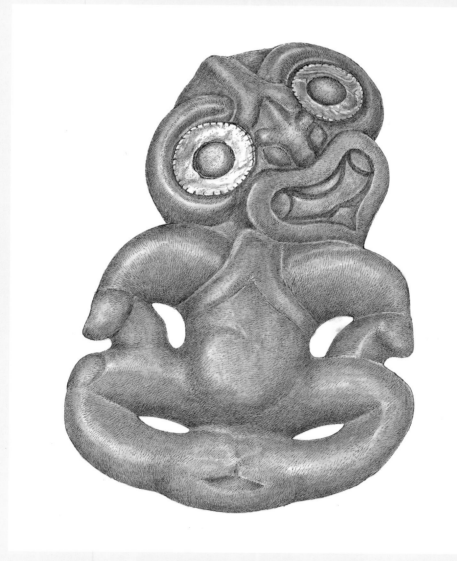

2.
New Zealand

41

3.
Australia

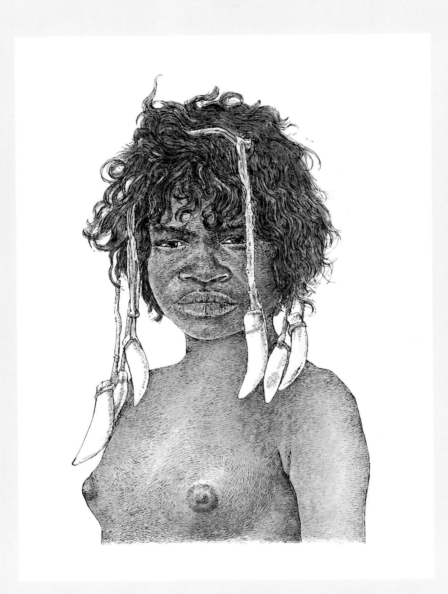

4.
Australia

5.
Solomon Islands/Melanesia

6. Solomon Islands

7. Solomon Islands

8. Solomon Islands

9. Santa-Cruz Island

10. Santa-Cruz Island

11. Solomon Islands

12. Papua New Guinea

13. Indonesia, West Irian

14.
Papua New Guinea

15.
Papua New Guinea

16.
Micronesia, Caroline Islands

17.
Micronesia, Truk Islands

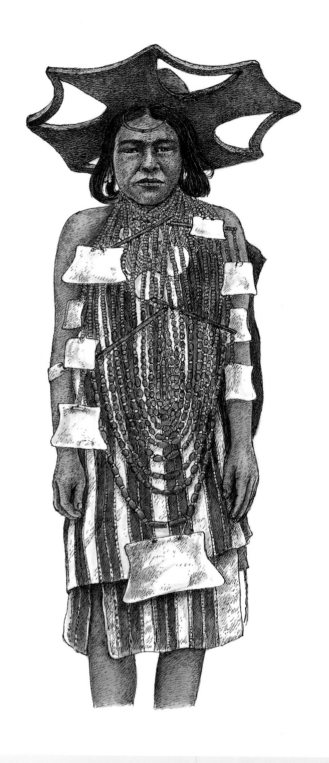

18.
Taiwan

19.
Taiwan

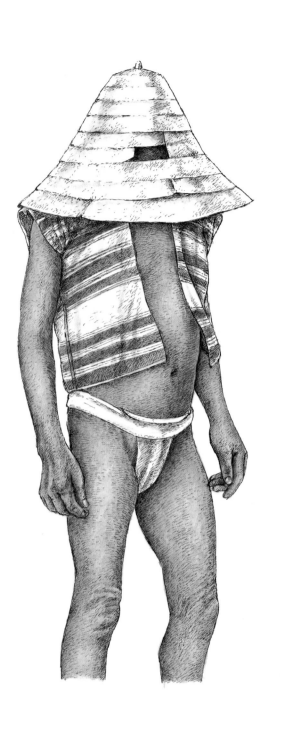

20.
Taiwan

21.
Taiwan

50

22.
Taiwan

23.
Taiwan

24.
Philippines

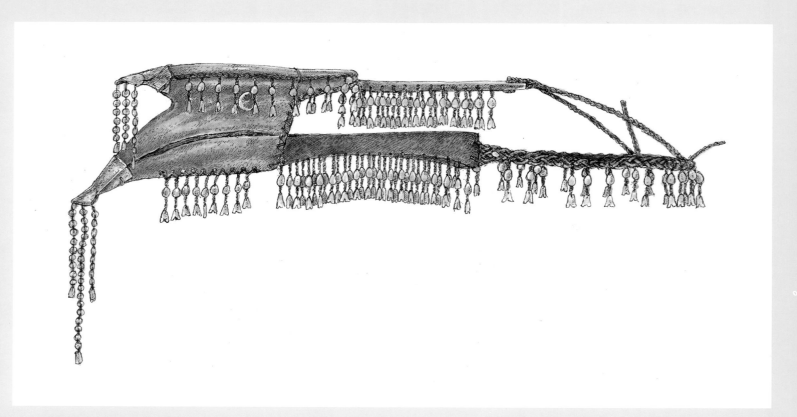

52   25. Philippines

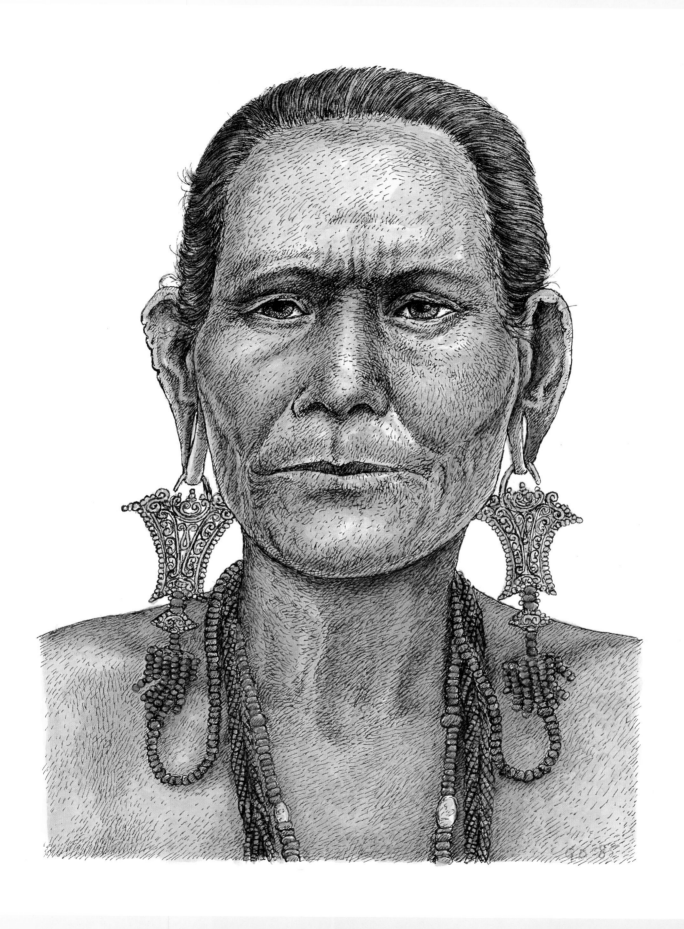

26.
Indonesia, Moluccas

54

29. Indonesia, Kalimantan

30. Malaysia, Sarawak

31. Indonesia, Kalimantan/Malaysia, Sarawak

32.
Malaysia, Sarawak

33. Indonesia, Kalimantan

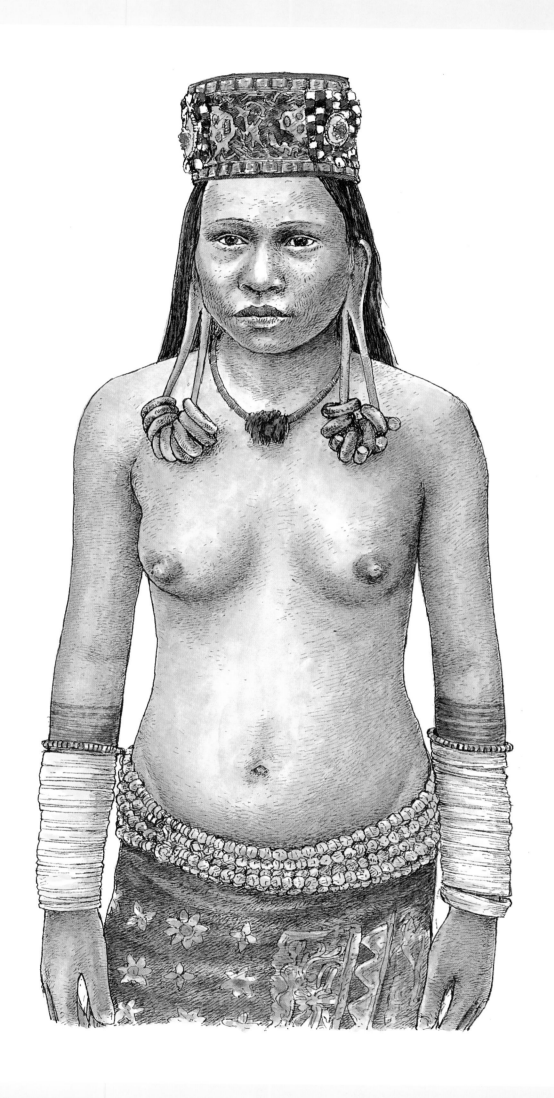

34. Indonesia, Kalimantan

35.
Indonesia, Nias

36.
Indonesia, Nias

37. Indonesia, Nias

38. Hainan

39. Hainan

40.
Vietnam/Southern China

41.
Vietnam

63

42.
Thailand

43.
Laos

44.
Thailand

45.
Thailand

46.
Burma/Thailand

47.
Thailand

48.
Thailand

49.
Burma

51. India

53. India   75

54. India

55. India

56. India

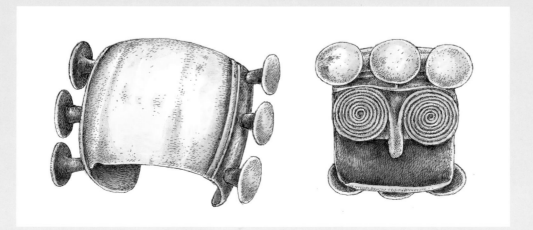

59. India

60. India

61. Sri Lanka

62. India

63.
India

64.
India

65.
India

66.
India/Nepal

67.
Nepal

68.
Nepal

85

69.
India, Ladakh

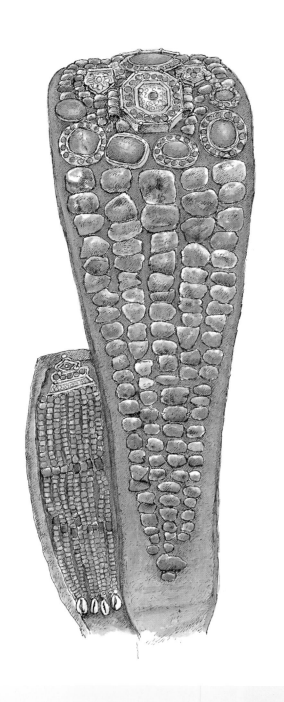

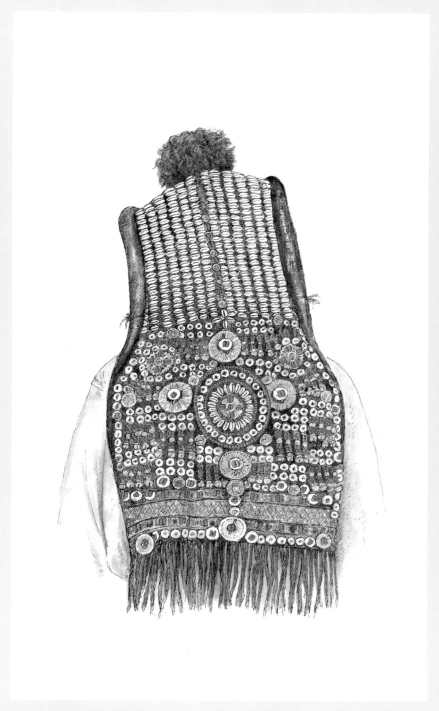

70.
India, Ladakh

71.
Pakistan

72. Tibet

73. Tibet

74. Tibet

75. Tibet

78. Tibet

79. Tibet

80. Tibet

93

81. Tibet

82. Tibet

85.
Tibet/China

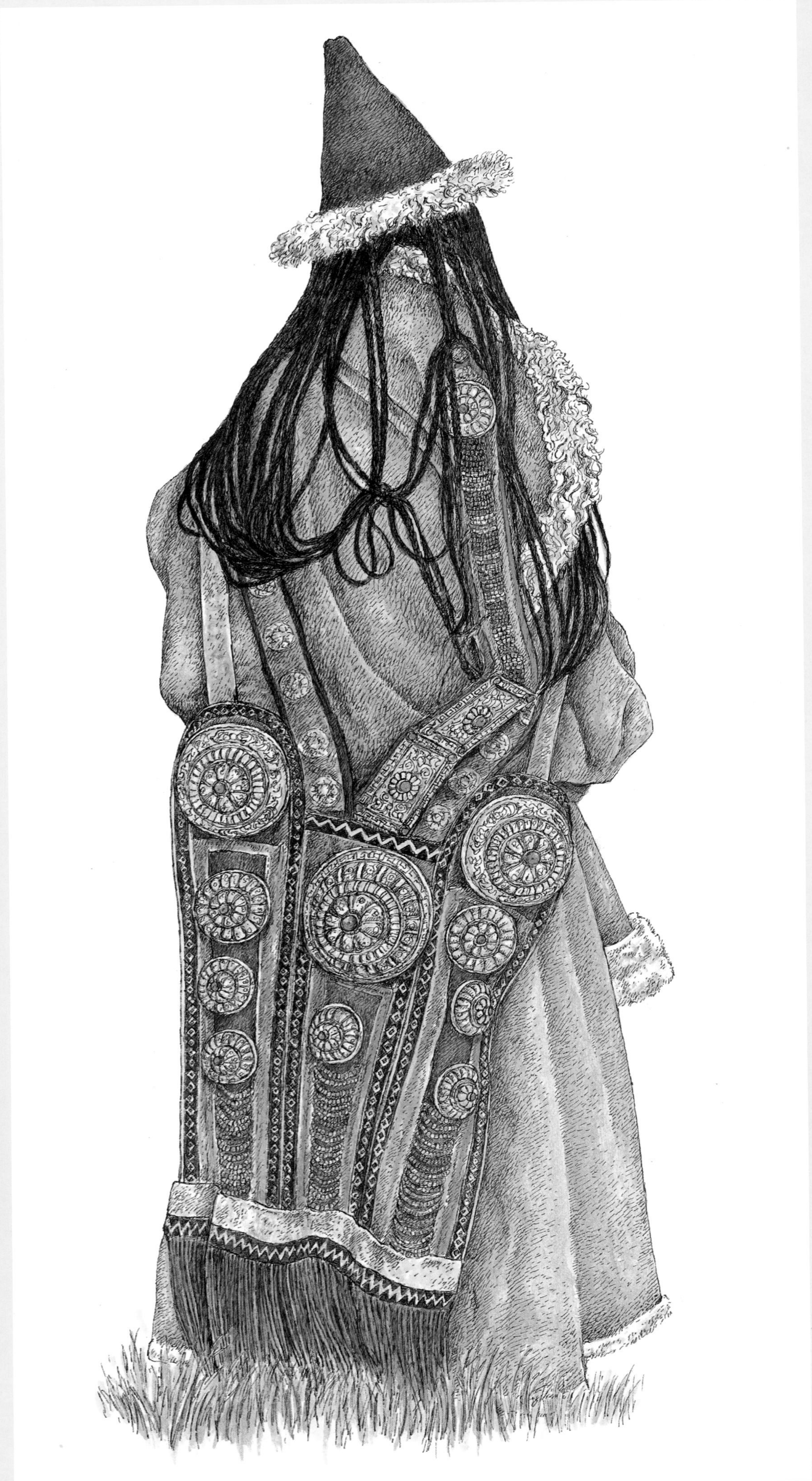

86.
Tibet/China

87.
Tibet/China

88.
Tibet/China

89.
Tibet/China

90.
Tibet/China

91. Tibet/China

92. Tibet/China

93.
Tibet/China

94.
Mongolia

95.
Mongolia

96.
Mongolia

97.
Mongolia

98.
Mongolia

100.
Mongolia

101.
Mongolia

102. Mongolia

103.
Mongolia

113

104
Mongolia

106. China

107. China

108. China

109. China

110. China

111. Japan

113.
Japan

114.
Japan

115.
Japan

116.
Japan

117.
Japan

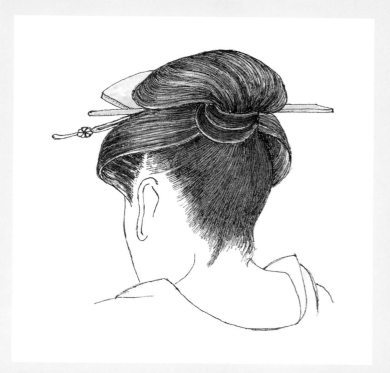

122   118. Central Asia, Kirgizia

119.
Central Asia/Soviet Union

120.
Central Asia/Iran

121.
Central Asia/Soviet Union

122. Central Asia/Soviet Union

123.
Central Asia/Iran

124.
Central Asia

126

125.
Central Asia/Soviet Union

126.
Central Asia/Afghanistan

127.
Central Asia/Soviet Union

128.
Central Asia/Soviet Union

129.
Central Asia/Soviet Union

130.
Central Asia/Soviet Union

131.
Central Asia/Iran

132.
Egypt

133.
Ethiopia

134.
Palestine

135.
Syria

136.
Algeria

137.
Algeria

138.
Algeria

139.
Algeria

140.
Sahara

143.
Mauretania

144.
Morocco

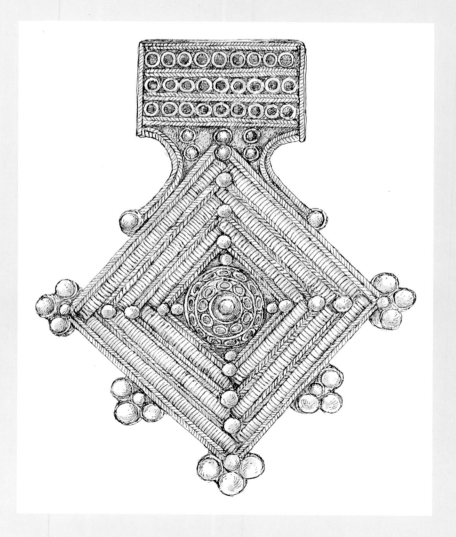

145.
Morocco

146. Niger/Sahara

147. Sahara

148. Niger/Sahara

143

149.
Morocco

150.
Morocco

151. Morocco

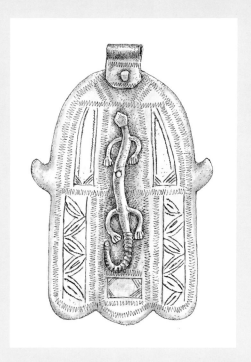

154.
Morocco

155.
Morocco

156.
Morocco

157.
Morocco

158.
Morocco

159.
Morocco

160.
Morocco

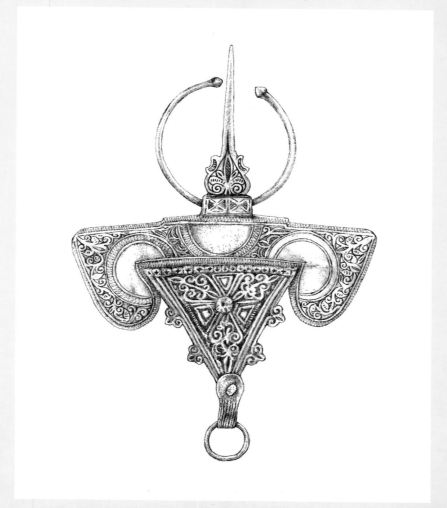

161.
Morocco

162.
Morocco

163.
Morocco

164.
Morocco

165.
Morocco

166.
Morocco

167.
Morocco

168.
Morocco

169.
Morocco

170.
Morocco

171.
Morocco

172.
Guinea-Bissau

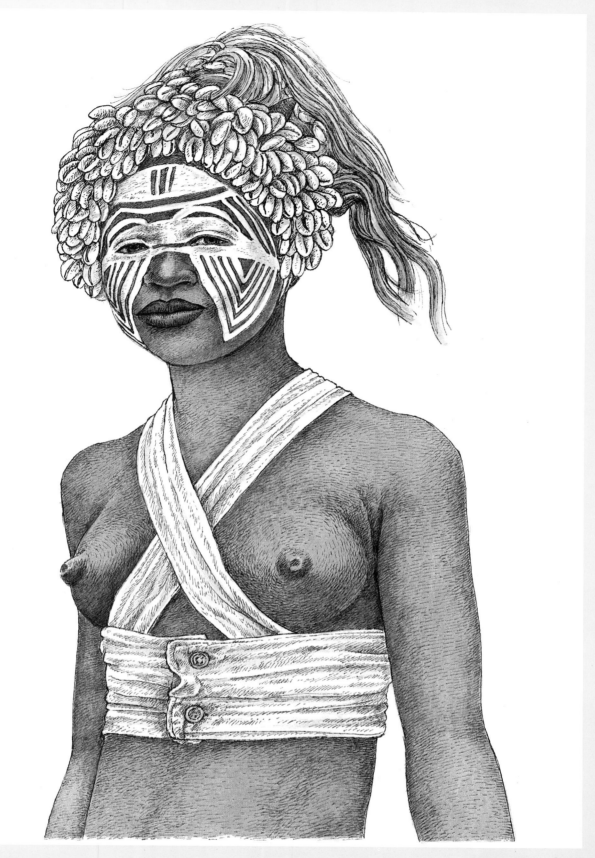

173.
Ivory Coast

174.
Zaire

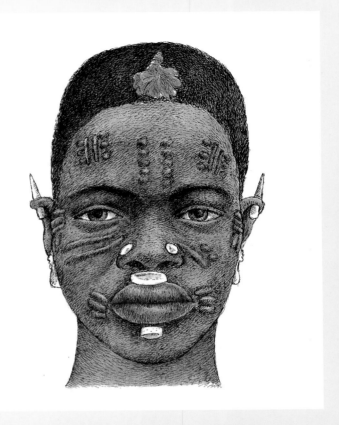

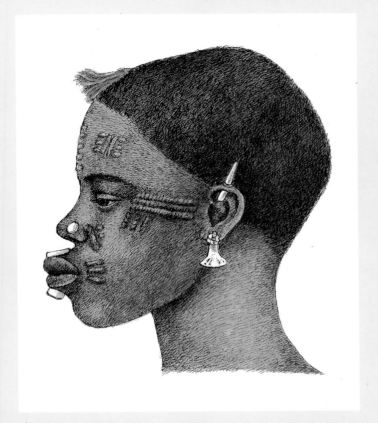

175. Cameroon

176. Cameroon

177.
Zaire

161

178. Angola

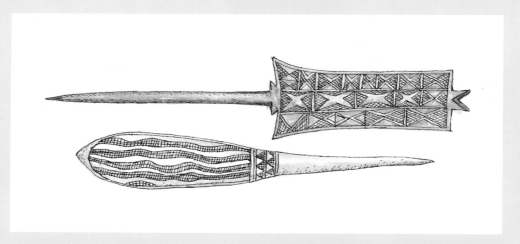

179.
Angola

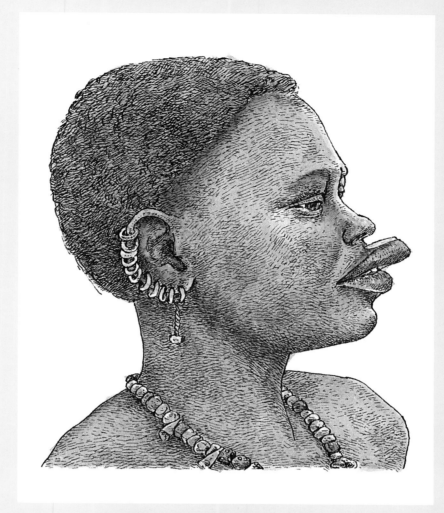

180.
Sudan

181.
Chad

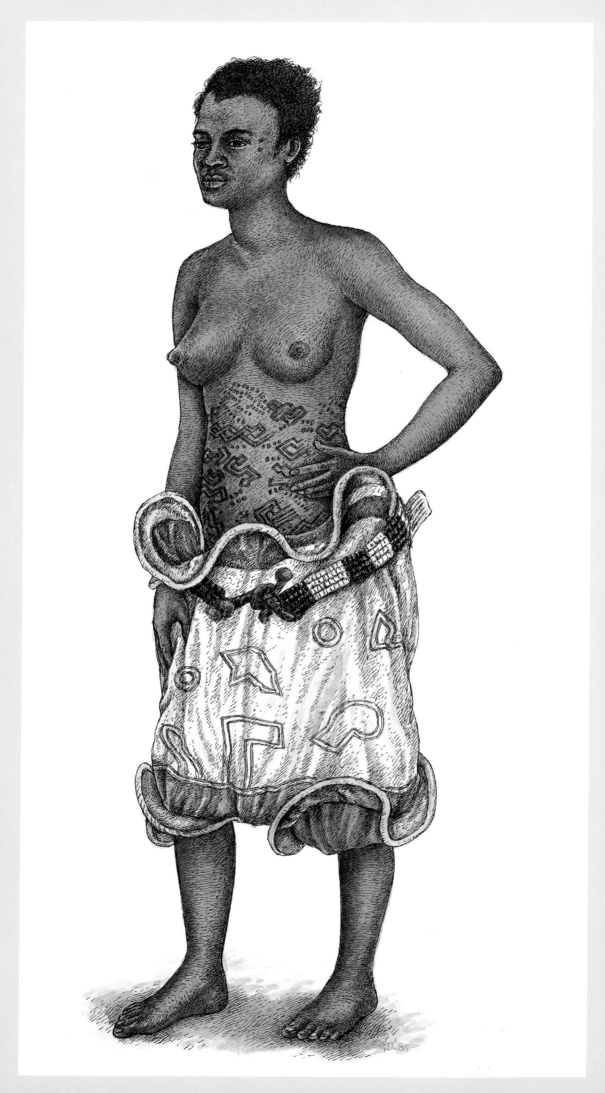

164   182. Zaire

183.
South Africa

184.
South Africa

185.
Niger

188.
Brazil

189.
Brazil

190.
Brazil

193. Brazil

194. Brazil

195.
Chile

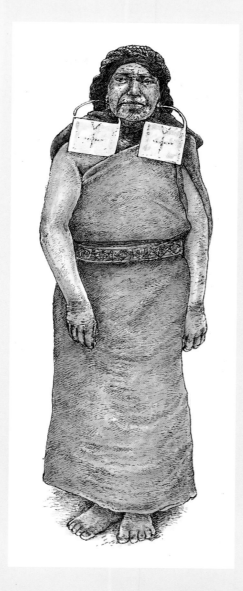

196.
Chile

197.
Chile

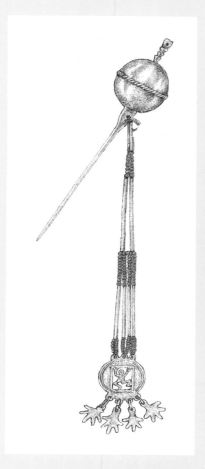

198.
Chile

199.
Bolivia

200. Chile

203.
Panama

204.
Mexico

205.
Guatemala

206.
Mexico

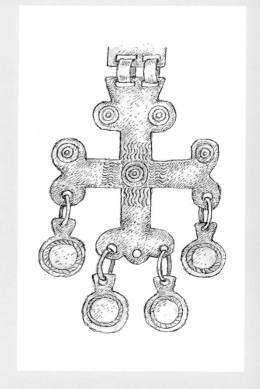

207. Mexico

208. Mexico

209. Chile

210.
Mexico

211.
Mexico

212.
Mexico

213.
United States

214.
United States

215.
United States

216.
United States

217.
United States

219.
United States

220.
United States

221.
Canada

222. Canada

223.
Greenland

224.
Canada

225.
Greenland

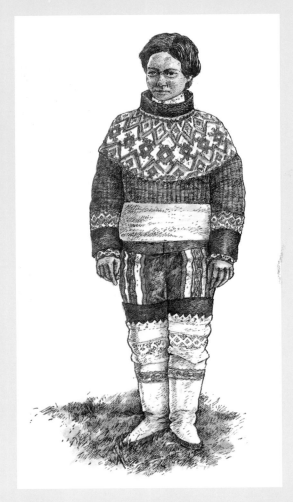

226.
Alaska

227.
Alaska

228.
Romania

229.
Russia (Europe)

230.
Russia (Europe)

233. Greece

234.
Romania

235.
Bulgaria

237.
Spain

238.
Germany

239.
Estonia

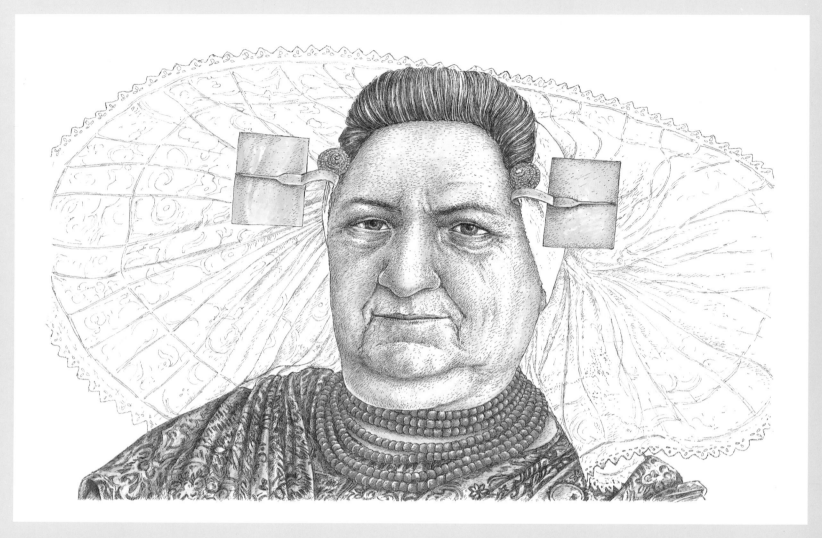

240. Netherlands

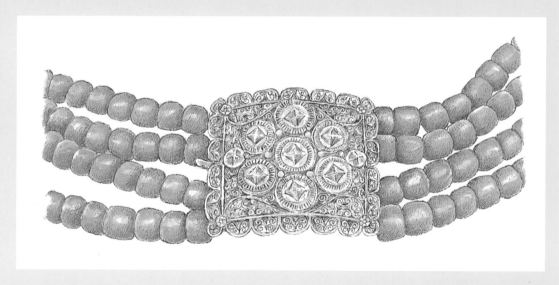

241.
Netherlands